ROUTE 66 TRAVEL & TOUR GUIDEBOOK 2024

"Unlock the Ultimate Route 66 Adventure Through Detailed Maps, Must-See Destinations, Accommodation & Dining Tips, and Step-by-Step Directions!"

BY

DAVID BROWN

Table of Contents

Introduction to Route 66

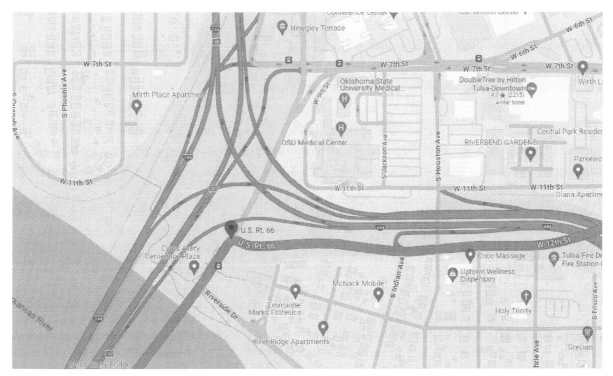

Route 66, often referred to as the "Main Street of America" or the "Will Rogers Highway," is a legendary highway that holds a special place in the hearts of travelers and enthusiasts alike. This historic route stretches across the United States, from Chicago, Illinois, in the east to Santa Monica, California, in the west, covering a distance of approximately 2,448 miles.

Originally established in 1926, Route 66 quickly became an iconic symbol of American freedom and adventure. It played a crucial role in connecting the nation, fostering economic growth, and facilitating westward migration during the early-to-mid 20th century.

In this travel guide, we embark on a journey along Route 66, not only to explore its rich history but also to uncover the hidden gems, cultural landmarks, and breathtaking landscapes that continue to captivate travelers today. Whether you're a history buff, a road trip enthusiast, or simply seeking an unforgettable travel experience, Route 66 has something to offer everyone.

This guide will take you mile by mile along the route, providing valuable insights, recommendations, and practical tips to help you make the most of your adventure. We'll delve into the history of Route 66, share stories of the people who lived and worked along the road, and guide you through planning a memorable journey on this iconic highway.

As we embark on this journey through time and place, let Route 66 be your gateway to a unique American experience. From the neon-lit streets of vintage diners to the quiet serenity of the open road, Route 66 promises adventure, nostalgia, and an enduring connection to the heart of America. So, fasten your seatbelt, roll down the windows, and let's hit the road on the historic Route 66. Your adventure awaits!

Purpose and Scope of the Guide

Welcome to the "Route 66 Travel & Tour Guide Book 2024." In this section, we'll outline the purpose and scope of this comprehensive guide to help you understand what to expect and how to make the most of your Route 66 adventure.

Purpose:

1. Inform and Inspire: This guide aims to inform and inspire travelers interested in exploring Route 66. Whether you're a first-time traveler or a seasoned road tripper, our goal is to provide you with the knowledge and inspiration to embark on a memorable journey.

2. Preserve Route 66's Legacy: Route 66 is more than just a road; it's a cultural and historical treasure. We're dedicated to preserving its legacy by sharing its history, significance, and the stories of the communities along the route.

3. Enhance the Travel Experience: We want to enhance your travel experience by offering valuable information on attractions, accommodations, dining, and safety tips. Our recommendations are designed to help you make the most of your time on Route 66.

4. Promote Responsible Travel: Responsible and sustainable travel is vital for the preservation of Route 66 and the well-being of the communities it passes through. We provide tips on how to travel responsibly and support local economies.

Scope:

1. Comprehensive Route Coverage: This guide covers Route 66 from its eastern terminus in Chicago, Illinois, to its western terminus in Santa Monica, California. We provide mile-by-mile details and highlight the most significant stops along the way.

2. Up-to-Date Information: The guide is current for the years 2024 and beyond, ensuring you have the latest information on attractions, accommodations, and events.

3. Variety of Travelers: We cater to a diverse audience, including solo travelers, families, history enthusiasts, adventure seekers, and culture lovers. You'll find information and recommendations suitable for different interests and travel styles.

4. Practical Tips: In addition to historical and cultural insights, we offer practical advice on trip planning, safety, budgeting, and sustainable travel practices.

5. Local Insights: We incorporate local perspectives and stories to provide a deeper understanding of the communities you'll encounter on your journey.

6. Side Trips and Extensions: While Route 66 is the main focus, we also suggest side trips and extensions to nearby attractions and scenic byways, allowing you to customize your adventure.

In summary, this guide is your comprehensive companion for experiencing the magic of Route 66 in 2024 and beyond. Whether you're looking for historical context, practical travel advice, or hidden gems along the route, we've got you covered. So, as you embark on your Route 66 adventure, let this guide be your trusted resource and source of inspiration. Enjoy the journey!

How to Use This Book

Navigating through the "Route 66 Travel & Tour Guide Book, 2024 Edition" is designed to be straightforward and user-friendly. Here's a guide on how to make the most of this book:

1. Start with the Table of Contents: Begin by reviewing the table of contents to get an overview of what the book offers. This will help you identify specific chapters or sections that are most relevant to your interests and needs.

2. Trip Planning: If you're in the early stages of planning your Route 66 adventure, start with Chapter 2, "Planning Your Route 66 Adventure." Here, you'll find guidance on choosing the right time to travel, creating a checklist, and budgeting for your trip.

3. Navigation: For practical navigation advice and a mile-by-mile guide, turn to Chapter 3, "Navigating the Route." It provides GPS coordinates, maps, and detailed directions to keep you on track.

4. Attractions and Landmarks: Discover the must-see attractions and hidden gems by exploring Chapter 4, "Attractions and Landmarks." It offers insights into the historical and cultural significance of various stops along Route 66.

5. Accommodations and Dining: Chapter 5, "Accommodations and Dining," is your go-to resource for finding places to stay and dine along the route. Whether you're looking for classic diners or cozy motels, you'll find recommendations here.

6. Roadside Americana: Explore the charm of classic diners, vintage gas stations, and quirky roadside attractions in Chapter 6, "Roadside Americana." It's a celebration of the nostalgia and character that defines Route 66.

7. Experiencing Local Culture: Chapter 7, "Experiencing Local Culture," introduces you to art, music festivals, and opportunities to connect with the local communities. Discover the unique cultural experiences that Route 66 offers.

8. Road Trip Tips and Safety: Prioritize safety and preparedness by reading Chapter 8, "Road Trip Tips and Safety." Learn about safety precautions, car maintenance, and what to do in emergencies.

9. Sustainability and Responsible Travel: Chapter 9, "Sustainability and Responsible Travel," provides insights on how to travel responsibly, reduce your environmental impact, and support local communities.

10. Beyond Route 66: If you're interested in extending your journey beyond Route 66, explore Chapter 10, "Beyond Route 66." It offers suggestions for side trips and connections to other scenic byways.

11. Route 66 in the Future: Gain insights into the preservation efforts, changing landscapes, and the future of Route 66 in Chapter 11, "Route 66 in the Future."

12. Copyright Information: Lastly, review the copyright information to understand usage and distribution rights.

Feel free to use this guide in a way that suits your travel style and interests. Whether you prefer to read it cover to cover or dip into specific chapters as needed, the goal is to enhance your Route 66 experience and make your journey as memorable as possible. Enjoy your adventure on the Main Street of America!

Chapter 1: Route 66 Overview

Welcome to the heart and soul of your Route 66 adventure. In this chapter, we embark on a journey of discovery as we delve into the fascinating history and enduring allure of the iconic Route 66. Often referred to as the "Main Street of America," this legendary highway has woven itself into the fabric of American culture, serving as a symbol of freedom, adventure, and the open road.

History and Evolution of Route 66

In the annals of American highways, few roads have achieved the legendary status and cultural significance of Route 66. The history and evolution of this iconic road are a captivating narrative of change, adventure, and nostalgia.

Early Beginnings:
In the early 20th century, the United States was undergoing a transformative period of industrialization and urbanization. With the rise of the automobile, the need for a well-structured highway system became increasingly apparent. It was clear that a reliable transcontinental road would not only facilitate the movement of goods and people but also stimulate economic growth and accessibility to the vast western territories.The concept of Route 66 emerged as a response to this need. In 1926, amid the rapid expansion of the U.S. highway system, Route 66 was officially designated as one of the nation's highways. Its original alignment stretched from Chicago, Illinois, in the east to Santa Monica, California, in the west, covering a distance of approximately 2,448 miles.

Route 66 was envisioned as a direct and efficient route, connecting the heartland of America, the Midwest, to the burgeoning communities on the West Coast. This highway soon earned the nickname "Main Street of America" due to its central role in uniting the nation, both geographically and economically.

The establishment of Route 66 marked a pivotal moment in American transportation history. It represented a commitment to infrastructure development and a symbol of progress during a time of profound change. Little did the early visionaries know that this highway would go on to become a cultural icon, capturing the imagination of generations to come and preserving the spirit of the American road trip.

As we journey along Route 66 today, it's important to reflect on these early beginnings and the visionaries who paved the way for this legendary road. Their foresight laid the foundation for the adventures, stories, and memories that travelers continue to create on this historic route.

The Dust Bowl and the Great Migration:
The 1930s brought unprecedented hardship to the American heartland. The Dust Bowl, a devastating ecological and agricultural crisis, left the Midwest in dire straits. Severe drought, coupled with poor farming practices, led to massive dust storms that ravaged the region. Fertile land turned to arid wastelands, crops failed, and families faced economic ruin. During this bleak period, Route 66 gained notoriety for an unexpected role—it became a lifeline for thousands of families in the Midwest. As the agricultural collapse deepened and jobs evaporated, desperate families looked westward for a glimmer of hope. Route 66, stretching from Chicago to the fertile lands of California, became the symbol of opportunity and a chance for a fresh start.

The mass migration westward along Route 66 during the Great Depression is vividly depicted in John Steinbeck's classic novel, "The Grapes of Wrath." Steinbeck's portrayal of the Joad family's journey along the highway captured the struggles, aspirations, and resilience of the Dust Bowl migrants. The novel brought national attention to the hardships faced by those seeking refuge along Route 66, and it contributed to the highway's reputation as the "Road to Opportunity." Route 66 became the path to a brighter future for many, even though the journey was fraught with challenges. Families loaded their belongings onto dilapidated vehicles, often with little more than hope in their hearts, and set out on the long and uncertain road westward. Along Route 66, they encountered kindness and support from strangers, as well as exploitation and adversity.

The highway was both a physical and symbolic conduit for these migrants, leading them to the promise of work and the dream of a better life in California. The struggles and triumphs of these Dust Bowl migrants, immortalized in literature and etched into the historical fabric of Route 66, remind us of the road's profound impact on the American experience.

World War II and the Mother Road:
During the tumultuous years of World War II, Route 66 assumed a role of paramount importance in the United States. This highway, already deeply woven into the fabric of American life, took on newfound significance as it became a vital artery for the transportation of troops, equipment, and supplies to support the war effort.

- Crucial Transportation Route:
Route 66's central location and well-maintained roads made it an ideal choice for military transport during World War II. Troops, tanks, aircraft, and other war materials were moved efficiently from one end of the country to the other using this highway. The road's reliability and accessibility earned it the nickname "The Road That Grew the Nation."

- Troops on the Move:
The highway saw a constant stream of military convoys and personnel heading westward. Soldiers, sailors, and airmen, en route to training bases, embarkation points, and ports of embarkation, experienced Route 66 as a symbol of transition—moving from civilian life to the rigors of wartime service.

- A Pause for Refreshment:
At the same time, the highway provided a respite for these servicemen. The roadside diners, motels, and cafes along Route 66 became places of comfort and solace, offering a taste of home to those far from their families and loved ones.

- Post-War Prosperity:

Following World War II, Route 66 experienced a post-war boom. Returning veterans and their families took to the highway in unprecedented numbers. This surge in travel marked the beginning of a golden era for Route 66, as it became the preferred route for those seeking adventure, leisure, and a slice of the American Dream.

- A Playground for Explorers:

Route 66 was more than just a means of transportation; it was a playground for explorers. Families embarked on cross-country road trips, creating lasting memories at the quirky roadside attractions, classic motels, and diners that had sprung up along the route.

The end of World War II marked a turning point in the history of Route 66. It had transitioned from a wartime lifeline to a symbol of post-war prosperity and exploration. The optimism and spirit of adventure that characterized this era continue to be associated with Route 66, making it not only an iconic highway but also a quintessential American experience.

As we travel the Mother Road today, we pay homage to its wartime significance and its role in shaping the American identity. Route 66 remains a tribute to the resilience of a nation and the enduring allure of the open road.

The Birth of Roadside Culture:

The 1950s and 1960s were a transformative period for Route 66, as this iconic highway gave birth to a distinctive roadside culture that has left an indelible mark on American travel history.

- Iconic Motels and Neon Signs:

One of the hallmarks of this era was the proliferation of motels along Route 66, each vying for the attention of passing travelers with their unique designs and eye-catching neon signs. These motels became more than just places to rest; they were works of art that reflected the exuberance of post-war America. Staying in a quaint motor court or a cozy cabin became an essential part of the Route 66 experience.

- Classic Diners and Drive-Ins:

Classic diners and drive-ins were the culinary stars of Route 66 during this period. These establishments offered not only delicious meals but also a nostalgic trip back in time. Road-weary travelers could savor burgers, milkshakes, and pie while seated at the counter, often in the company of locals who frequented these cherished community gathering spots.

- Quirky Roadside Attractions:

Route 66 embraced the eccentric and the whimsical, with quirky roadside attractions capturing the imaginations of travelers. Giant fiberglass statues, novelty museums, and mysterious landmarks peppered the route, inviting adventurers to take a break from the road and explore the unexpected.

- Leisurely Road Trips and Adventure:

The 1950s and 1960s saw an explosion of leisurely road trips along Route 66. Families piled into cars and set out on adventures, creating cherished memories as they explored the diverse landscapes and attractions of the American Southwest. Route 66 became synonymous with carefree exploration and the joy of discovery.

- The Mother Road in Pop Culture:

During this period, Route 66's cultural prominence extended beyond the road itself. It inspired songs, literature, and television series, most notably the popular TV show "Route 66." This series followed the adventures of two young men exploring the country in their Corvette along Route 66, further romanticizing the highway in the eyes of the American public.

The 1950s and 1960s were a golden era for Route 66, a time when the highway was not just a means of travel but a destination in itself. It was a place where travelers could experience the essence of American culture, from roadside diners to kitschy attractions, all while immersing themselves in the unique spirit of the open road. Today, as we travel Route 66, we continue to celebrate and preserve this vibrant roadside culture. The classic motels, neon signs, and roadside relics that remain serve as a living testament to the enduring charm and nostalgia of this iconic highway.

Decline and Decommissioning:

The 1960s marked a turning point in the history of Route 66, as the construction of the Interstate Highway System began to divert traffic away from this once-thriving highway. This period of decline and the eventual decommissioning of Route 66 in 1985 marked the end of an era but also initiated a dedicated preservation movement to protect its cultural heritage.

- Impact of the Interstate Highway System:

The construction and expansion of the Interstate Highway System in the mid-20th century brought about a fundamental shift in American transportation. These new, high-speed, limited-access highways were designed for efficiency and faster travel, often bypassing the smaller towns and businesses that had thrived along Route 66. This diversion of traffic had a profound impact on the businesses and communities that depended on the road for their livelihoods.

- Decline of Businesses:

As traffic dwindled on Route 66, businesses along the route struggled to survive. Motels, diners, and roadside attractions that had once flourished now faced economic hardship. Many of these establishments were forced to close their doors, and the once-bustling road began to show signs of neglect.

- Decommissioning of Route 66:

In 1985, Route 66 was officially decommissioned as a U.S. highway. This decision marked the end of its role as a primary transportation route and signaled a shift in the way Americans traveled. With its removal from the U.S. highway system, Route 66 ceased to receive federal funding for maintenance and improvements.

- Birth of the Preservation Movement:

The decommissioning of Route 66 was met with nostalgia and a sense of loss among those who cherished its history and cultural significance. In response, a grassroots preservation movement emerged, dedicated to saving and restoring the landmarks, signs, and memories associated with Route 66.

- Preservation and Revival Efforts:

Throughout the late 20th century and into the 21st century, passionate individuals, communities, and organizations worked tirelessly to preserve and revive Route 66. Historic preservation projects, museum exhibits, and initiatives to restore iconic roadside attractions helped breathe new life into the Mother Road.

- Designation as a National Scenic Byway:

In recognition of its historical and cultural importance, many states along Route 66 designated segments of the highway as state scenic byways. In 2008, the route was officially designated a National Scenic Byway, reaffirming its significance as a cultural and historic icon.

Today, Route 66 has been partially resurrected as a symbol of American nostalgia and adventure. Travelers from around the world embark on pilgrimages along its path, seeking to connect with the past and experience the unique charm of the road. The preservation of its heritage serves as a testament to the enduring allure of Route 66 and the dedication of those who refuse to let its memory fade. It remains a testament to the resilience of the Mother Road and the enduring spirit of the communities that call it home.

Revival and Preservation:

Recent decades have witnessed a remarkable resurgence of interest in Route 66, as enthusiasts, communities, and preservationists have united to breathe new life into this iconic highway. This revival and preservation movement have helped ensure that the legacy of Route 66 endures for future generations.

- Community-Led Restoration:

One of the most inspiring aspects of the Route 66 revival has been the dedication of local communities and businesses to preserve the highway's heritage. Many towns along the route have undertaken restoration projects to revitalize classic motels, diners, gas stations, and roadside attractions. These efforts have helped recapture the nostalgic charm of Route 66.

- <u>Historic Landmarks and Museums:</u>

Across the length of the highway, you'll find historic landmarks and museums dedicated to preserving the history of Route 66. These institutions celebrate the road's significance and showcase artifacts, memorabilia, and stories that pay tribute to its past. They provide travelers with valuable insights into the road's history and cultural impact.

- <u>Route 66 Associations:</u>

Route 66 associations have sprung up in various states, serving as advocacy groups dedicated to preserving and promoting the highway. These organizations work to raise awareness, secure funding for restoration projects, and organize events that celebrate Route 66's heritage.

- <u>Designation as a National Scenic Byway:</u>

Route 66's cultural and historical importance was officially recognized when it was designated a National Scenic Byway by the U.S. government. This designation highlights the highway's scenic, cultural, and historic value, drawing attention to its role as a quintessential American road trip experience.

- <u>Festivals and Events:</u>

Numerous Route 66 festivals and events take place annually, attracting travelers and enthusiasts from around the world. These gatherings celebrate the road's history, culture, and vibrant community spirit. They offer opportunities for live music, car shows, parades, and more, creating a sense of camaraderie among those who share a passion for the Mother Road.

- <u>Preserving the Spirit of the Open Road:</u>

The revival and preservation efforts surrounding Route 66 serve a dual purpose: safeguarding the highway's history and cultural heritage while also providing a roadmap for future generations to experience the spirit of the open road. Travelers today can embark on their own journeys along Route 66, connecting with the past and forging new memories.

As you travel Route 66 today, you'll have the chance to witness the fruits of these preservation and revival efforts firsthand. The dedication of countless individuals and communities ensures that the legacy of Route 66 remains vibrant and accessible, inviting you to explore a unique piece of American history and culture.

Route 66 Today:

In the 21st century, Route 66 stands as a living testament to the enduring allure of the American road trip. While it may no longer be the primary artery for cross-country travel, it has evolved into a symbol of adventure, freedom, and nostalgia that continues to captivate travelers from around the world.

- A Pilgrimage of Nostalgia:

For many, traveling Route 66 has become a pilgrimage of nostalgia—a journey back in time to an era when the open road represented boundless possibilities. The highway's preserved motels, diners, and roadside attractions offer a tangible connection to the past, allowing travelers to relive the experiences of generations before them.

- A Taste of Americana:

Route 66 is a portal to the heart of Americana. Along its storied path, you'll encounter classic diners serving up hearty meals, neon-lit motels that harken back to the golden age of road trips, and quirky roadside attractions that defy expectations. These experiences provide a taste of the cultural and culinary tapestry that defines American life.

- A Sense of Freedom:

Route 66 embodies the spirit of freedom that road trips represent. The open road stretches out endlessly before you, offering the freedom to choose your own path, explore at your own pace, and uncover hidden gems along the way. It's a journey that encourages spontaneity and adventure.

- Cultural and Historical Connection:

Route 66 serves as a tangible link to America's past. It's a road that witnessed the struggles of Dust Bowl migrants, played a vital role in World War II, and thrived during the post-war boom. Travelers today can connect with these historical events and gain a deeper understanding of the nation's heritage.

- <u>New Generations of Road Trippers:</u>

While Route 66 holds a special place in the hearts of those who remember its heyday, it continues to captivate new generations of road trippers and history enthusiasts. The enduring legacy of the highway ensures that its spirit will be carried forward by those who seek to experience the magic of the open road.

As you embark on your own Route 66 journey, understanding its history and evolution adds depth to the adventure. Each mile of this iconic road is infused with stories, landmarks, and a sense of timelessness that beckons you to explore its winding path through the heartland of America.

The Significance of Route 66 in American Culture

Route 66 holds a profound and enduring significance in American culture, transcending its role as a mere highway to become a symbol of freedom, adventure, and the American Dream. Its cultural importance can be understood through several key facets:

1. Icon of Freedom:

Route 66 stands as a quintessential icon of American freedom, encapsulating the very essence of the nation's pioneering spirit. This highway is more than just a stretch of asphalt; it symbolizes the open road and all the boundless opportunities it represents. The concept of freedom has long been woven into the American identity. Route 66 personifies this ideal by offering a physical manifestation of the freedom to travel, explore, and chart one's own course. It beckons travelers to leave behind the constraints of daily life and venture into the unknown, echoing the spirit of early American pioneers who embarked on westward journeys into uncharted territories.

As travelers traverse Route 66, they experience the thrill of exploration and the promise of new horizons. The road's expansive vistas, diverse landscapes, and intriguing roadside attractions evoke a sense of wonder and possibility. This connection with the open road mirrors the adventurous spirit that has driven Americans to explore the frontier, build communities, and strive for a better future throughout the nation's history. In a world that often feels increasingly interconnected and regulated, Route 66 remains a symbol of unbridled freedom—a reminder that the American dream still includes the pursuit of adventure and the open road. It continues to resonate with individuals who yearn to break free from the routine, embrace the unknown, and celebrate the enduring spirit of exploration that defines the American character.

2. Historical Threads:

Route 66 serves as a tangible thread that weaves through the historical fabric of America, bearing witness to pivotal events and embodying the resilience and progress of the nation. The highway's historical significance is deeply interwoven with key moments in American history. During the Great Depression, Route 66 gained prominence as the path of escape for thousands of families fleeing the Dust Bowl's devastating ecological and economic hardships. The mass migration westward, often referred to as the "Okie migration," turned Route 66 into a lifeline for those seeking refuge and a new beginning. The highway became a symbol of hope and opportunity during a time of profound adversity.

World War II saw Route 66 assume a crucial role as a vital transportation route. Troops, equipment, and supplies were transported efficiently along this highway, solidifying its place in the American psyche. The highway's reliability and accessibility made it an indispensable asset in supporting the war effort. Post-war, Route 66 took on new significance as it symbolized the nation's post-war prosperity and the promise of a brighter future. Returning soldiers and their families hit the open road, seeking adventure and the realization of the American Dream. The highway became a symbol of the nation's collective optimism, as it represented the freedom to explore and pursue a better life.

These historical events have become an integral part of the American narrative, with Route 66 serving as a tangible link to the past. Traveling this highway today allows us to connect with the struggles and triumphs of those who came before us. It's a reminder of the resilience of individuals and communities during challenging times and a celebration of the enduring spirit of the American people. Route 66's historical threads continue to be a source of inspiration and reflection, reminding us of the nation's ability to overcome adversity and build a better future.

3. Roadside Culture:

Route 66 is not just a road; it's a cultural phenomenon that blossomed in the mid-20th century and remains an integral part of its enduring legacy. The highway's unique roadside culture is a quintessential aspect of Route 66's identity, characterized by classic diners, neon-lit motels, and quirky attractions that have captivated generations of travelers.

One of the most iconic elements of Route 66's roadside culture is the classic American diner. Along the route, you'll find diners that have stood the test of time, serving up hearty meals and nostalgia in equal portions. These diners, often with their retro interiors and welcoming counters, invite travelers to experience the authentic flavors of the past while forging new memories.

The neon-lit motels that dot Route 66 have become symbols of the open road's allure. These vintage accommodations, adorned with vibrant signs, harken back to the golden age of road trips. Staying in a Route 66 motel is not merely a practical choice but an immersion into a bygone era of travel, where comfort and character coexist. Quirky attractions are another hallmark of Route 66's roadside culture. The highway is home to a variety of eccentric landmarks, from giant fiberglass statues to novelty museums and mysterious curiosities. These attractions have a magnetic quality, drawing travelers off the road to explore the unexpected and add an element of surprise to their journey.

The roadside culture of Route 66 represents a snapshot of mid-20th-century America. It reflects the nation's fascination with the automobile, leisurely travel, and the desire for adventure. It's a culture that continues to captivate travelers, offering them a chance to step back in time and experience the authenticity of the American road trip.

Today, as travelers embark on their own Route 66 adventures, they have the opportunity to embrace and celebrate this unique roadside culture. It's a culture that encourages nostalgia, curiosity, and a deep appreciation for the enduring charm of classic diners, neon signs, and the quirky attractions that define the Mother Road's cultural tapestry.

4. Literary and Pop Culture:

Route 66's influence extends beyond the asphalt, leaving an indelible mark on American literature and pop culture. It has inspired and been immortalized in various forms of artistic expression, including acclaimed novels and popular television series, highlighting its enduring cultural significance.

One of the most notable literary works associated with Route 66 is John Steinbeck's "The Grapes of Wrath." Published in 1939, this Pulitzer Prize-winning novel vividly portrays the struggles of the Joad family as they journey along Route 66 during the Dust Bowl migration. Steinbeck's narrative serves as a powerful commentary on the hardships faced by those who sought refuge and hope along the highway. "The Grapes of Wrath" not only became a literary classic but also contributed to Route 66's reputation as the "Road to Opportunity."

In the realm of television, the series "Route 66" left an indelible mark on pop culture. Airing from 1960 to 1964, the show followed the adventures of two young men traveling the country in their Corvette along Route 66. Each episode offered a glimpse into the diverse landscapes, characters, and stories encountered along the highway. "Route 66" captured the imagination of viewers and further romanticized the allure of the open road, solidifying the highway's place in American pop culture. Beyond these notable examples, Route 66 has been referenced, celebrated, and depicted in a myriad of books, songs, films, and artworks. Its iconic status as the "Main Street of America" and its role as a symbol of the American road trip have made it a source of inspiration for artists and storytellers alike. The highway's presence in literature and pop culture continues to resonate with audiences, connecting them with the highway's rich history and cultural significance.

5. Symbol of Resilience:

Route 66's journey from decline to preservation is a testament to the resilience of communities and the unwavering dedication of individuals to safeguard cultural heritage. This transformation serves as a poignant reminder that even in the face of adversity, cultural treasures can be preserved, celebrated, and given new life.

When Route 66 faced decline due to the construction of the Interstate Highway System in the 1960s, it was the communities along the route that felt the impact most profoundly. Many businesses struggled, and the highway's importance as a transportation route diminished. Yet, instead of succumbing to the challenges, these communities rallied together, demonstrating remarkable resilience.

The preservation movement that emerged was driven by a shared commitment to protecting the cultural heritage embodied by Route 66. Local residents, business owners, historians, and enthusiasts worked tirelessly to ensure that the highway's landmarks, signs, and stories were not lost to history. Their efforts often involved restoring classic motels, neon signs, and iconic roadside attractions to their former glory. These preservation endeavors extended beyond physical restoration. Museums and historical societies were established to collect and curate the artifacts, photographs, and memories associated with Route 66. These institutions served as repositories of the highway's rich history, ensuring that its legacy would be passed down to future generations.

Today, Route 66 stands as a living testament to the determination of these preservationists. The highway's designation as a National Scenic Byway, state scenic byways in various regions, and the continued appeal to tourists from around the world all underscore the successful preservation efforts. Route 66 has been revitalized as a symbol of the enduring spirit of the communities that call it home and a reminder that cultural treasures can be saved and celebrated, even in the face of challenges. As travelers journey along Route 66 today, they bear witness to the resilience of those who refused to let its memory fade. They connect with a living history that serves as a shining example of how communities can come together to protect their cultural heritage, ensuring that Route 66 remains an integral part of the American narrative for generations to come.

6. Tourist Attraction:
Route 66 has not only retained its cultural significance but has also evolved into a thriving tourist attraction that magnetizes visitors from both within the United States and abroad. Today, the highway serves as a living time capsule, offering travelers a unique opportunity to experience a slice of American nostalgia and

explore the diverse landscapes and communities along its path. Domestic and international tourists alike are drawn to Route 66, embarking on journeys that often become lifelong memories. The highway's enduring appeal lies in its ability to transport travelers back in time, allowing them to relive the bygone era of mid-20th-century America. The classic diners, neon-lit motels, and quirky roadside attractions provide a sense of nostalgia and authenticity that is increasingly rare in the modern world.

The international allure of Route 66 is noteworthy. Travelers from around the globe are captivated by the mystique of the American road trip, which has been romanticized in literature, film, and music. For many, Route 66 represents the embodiment of that dream—a chance to explore the vastness of the United States while immersing themselves in its culture and history.

The tourism industry along Route 66 has grown in response to this demand. Classic motels, bed-and-breakfasts, and boutique hotels cater to travelers seeking an authentic experience. Gift shops and memorabilia stores offer souvenirs that celebrate the highway's heritage. Festivals and events dedicated to Route 66 draw crowds, fostering a sense of community and celebration.

While Route 66's role as a primary transportation route has waned, its role as a tourist attraction has flourished. The highway's designation as a National Scenic Byway and its recognition as a symbol of American nostalgia have further solidified its status as a must-visit destination for travelers seeking adventure, history, and a taste of the open road.

Today, travelers become part of a thriving tourism industry that celebrates the highway's unique cultural and historical significance. The experience of traversing this iconic route not only connects them with the past but also offers a chance to create new memories that will forever be associated with the allure of Route 66.

7. A Living History:
Travelers who embark on the legendary Route 66 journey become integral participants in a living history. Their experiences extend beyond the mere act of travel; they connect with the stories, memories, and enduring spirit of those who

traversed this iconic road before them. In doing so, they simultaneously forge new adventures while paying homage to the past. Route 66, often referred to as the "Main Street of America," has borne witness to generations of travelers. As you journey along its path, you follow in the footsteps of Dust Bowl migrants seeking refuge, World War II troops on vital missions, post-war families in pursuit of the American Dream, and countless other individuals who have left their mark on the highway's narrative.

The highway's landmarks, museums, and preserved sites serve as portals to the past, offering travelers the opportunity to delve into the rich history of Route 66. These stops not only provide insights into the challenges and triumphs of those who came before but also allow you to appreciate the enduring cultural and historical significance of the highway. Yet, Route 66 is more than just a historical relic. It's a road that encourages new adventures and creates fresh memories for each traveler who embarks on the journey. The open road stretches before you, offering the freedom to choose your own path, explore at your own pace, and discover hidden treasures along the way.

As you traverse Route 66, you become a custodian of its legacy. Your journey adds to the collective tapestry of experiences, stories, and memories associated with the highway. You honor the resilience of the communities that have preserved its heritage and celebrate the enduring spirit of exploration that Route 66 embodies. In essence, Route 66 is a bridge between the past and the present, where the road itself becomes a living history book. It invites travelers to embrace the stories of yesterday while creating their own chapters, forging connections with the past and inspiring future generations to follow in the tire tracks of those who have come before.

Modern-Day Relevance

While Route 66 may be steeped in nostalgia and history, its modern-day relevance remains strikingly vibrant. This iconic highway continues to resonate with a wide range of individuals and communities, and it holds enduring importance for several reasons in the contemporary world:

1. Tourism and Economic Impact: Route 66's status as a top tourist attraction bolsters local economies along its path. Travelers contribute to the economic vitality of communities by staying in accommodations, dining in restaurants, and purchasing souvenirs. The tourism industry that Route 66 sustains helps support businesses and jobs in these regions.

2. Cultural Preservation: The preservation of Route 66's cultural heritage remains essential in the modern era. As historical sites and attractions are maintained, they provide educational opportunities for both locals and visitors, fostering an appreciation for America's past. This cultural preservation safeguards the legacy of the highway for future generations.

3. Historical Education: Route 66 offers a unique lens through which to view American history. As a living history lesson, it allows travelers to connect with significant events like the Dust Bowl migration and World War II. In today's educational landscape, Route 66 continues to serve as a valuable resource for teaching history and culture.

4. Community Identity: Communities along Route 66 often derive a sense of identity and pride from their connection to the highway. Local festivals, events, and cultural initiatives centered around Route 66 help foster a sense of community and belonging, even in the face of modern challenges.

5. Environmental Awareness: In an age of environmental consciousness, Route 66 represents a more leisurely and environmentally friendly mode of travel compared to highways with heavy congestion. It encourages a slower pace of exploration, providing an opportunity to appreciate the natural beauty and heritage of the regions through which it passes.

6. Preservation Advocacy: Route 66's ongoing preservation efforts demonstrate the power of grassroots movements and community activism. This serves as a modern-day reminder that individuals and communities can unite to protect and celebrate their cultural treasures.

7. Cultural Exchange: International travelers continue to flock to Route 66, fostering cultural exchange and global understanding. The highway serves as a bridge connecting people from diverse backgrounds who share a common fascination with American culture and history.

In summary, Route 66 remains a symbol of resilience, community, and cultural heritage in the modern world. Its continued relevance underscores the enduring appeal of the open road, the importance of preserving historical treasures, and the potential for communities to thrive by embracing their unique histories and identities. Route 66 is not simply a relic of the past; it's a dynamic and enduring part of America's cultural landscape.

Chapter 2: Planning Your Route 66 Adventure

As you prepare to embark on your Route 66 adventure, it's essential to understand the modern-day relevance of this iconic highway. While Route 66 is steeped in history and nostalgia, it continues to thrive in the contemporary world, offering travelers a unique blend of culture, history, and exploration. In this chapter, I'll explore the reasons why Route 66 remains a captivating journey for enthusiasts from around the world and provide you with practical insights to plan a memorable and meaningful adventure along the Mother Road. Whether you're drawn to its cultural significance, historical education, or the economic impact it has on local communities, Route 66 has something to offer every traveler. So, let's dive into the planning process and uncover the secrets of this enduring American treasure.

Choosing the Right Time to Travel

Selecting the ideal time for your Route 66 adventure is a crucial step in ensuring a memorable and enjoyable journey. The timing of your trip can significantly impact your experience, from the weather you'll encounter to the availability of accommodations and attractions along the route. Here are some key factors to consider when deciding when to travel Route 66:

- **1. Weather Considerations:**
When planning your Route 66 adventure, one of the foremost factors to weigh is the weather. The climate along the route can be diverse, so understanding seasonal patterns and their impact on your journey is vital.

a. Summer Heat:
Summer along Route 66, particularly in the southwestern states like Arizona and New Mexico, can be scorching. High temperatures, often exceeding 100°F (37.8°C), can make outdoor activities uncomfortable, especially for extended periods. Travelers who can tolerate the heat may find fewer crowds and vibrant summer festivals during this season.

b. Chilly Winters:

On the flip side, winter brings cooler and sometimes cold conditions, especially in the northern states like Illinois and Missouri. While you might encounter fewer tourists, you'll need to prepare for potentially icy roads and the occasional road closure due to snowstorms. However, if you enjoy winter activities and don't mind bundling up, this season can offer a unique perspective of Route 66.

c. Spring and Fall Bliss:

Spring and fall are often considered the sweet spots for traveling Route 66. During these seasons, temperatures are more moderate, ranging from pleasantly warm in spring to comfortably cool in fall. This weather allows for more enjoyable outdoor exploration and activities. Additionally, spring brings blooming wildflowers, while fall offers vibrant foliage, enhancing the scenic beauty along the route.

d. Regional Variations:

Keep in mind that weather conditions can vary significantly by region. For instance, the desert landscapes of the Southwest can be scorching in summer but pleasant in winter, while the Midwest may experience milder summers but harsher winters. Research the weather patterns specific to the areas you plan to visit to make informed decisions.

Ultimately, your choice of travel time should align with your comfort level in various weather conditions. Whether you prefer the sizzle of summer, the coziness of winter, or the mild appeal of spring and fall, understanding the seasonal climate will help ensure your Route 66 adventure is as enjoyable as possible.

- **2. Crowds and Availability:**

When planning your Route 66 adventure, consider the impact of crowds and the availability of accommodations on your overall experience. Timing your trip can significantly influence the level of congestion and the ease of securing lodging along the route.

a. Summer Crowds:

Peak tourist season along Route 66 coincides with the summer months, particularly from June to August. During this period, you can expect larger crowds at popular attractions, diners, and motels. While summer offers vibrant festivals and events, it's essential to book accommodations well in advance, as they are in high demand. Be prepared for potentially longer wait times at attractions and restaurants.

b. Spring and Fall Tranquility:
Traveling during the shoulder seasons of spring and fall can provide a more relaxed and peaceful experience. Crowds tend to be thinner, making it easier to explore attractions without the hustle and bustle. Booking accommodations may also be less competitive, offering more flexibility in your travel plans. These seasons often boast milder weather, enhancing the overall comfort of your journey.

c. Consider Weekdays:
Regardless of the season, weekdays generally see fewer tourists than weekends. If your schedule allows, planning your Route 66 adventure to include weekdays can help you avoid weekend crowds and potentially secure accommodations with greater ease.

d. Event Impact:
Route 66 hosts numerous events and festivals throughout the year. While these gatherings can add excitement to your journey, they may also affect crowd levels and accommodation availability. Research the event calendar along the route to align your travel plans with events that interest you.

In summary, the timing of your Route 66 adventure should factor in your preference for crowd levels and accommodation availability. While summer offers lively festivities, consider the shoulder seasons for a more relaxed and less congested experience. Additionally, planning your trip to include weekdays can further enhance your enjoyment of the Mother Road.

- **3. Special Events and Festivals:**
The vibrant pulse of Route 66 is often best felt during its myriad events and festivals, which provide travelers an immersive experience into the heart and soul of this iconic highway.

a. Diverse Celebrations:

Throughout the year, Route 66 comes alive with a plethora of events that celebrate its rich history and unique culture. From classic car shows that harken back to the golden age of automobiles to music festivals that echo with the sounds of Americana, there's a wealth of gatherings that encapsulate the essence of the Mother Road. Each event offers a snapshot of the communities, traditions, and stories that make Route 66 legendary.

b. Historical Deep Dive:

For history enthusiasts, events like historical reenactments or heritage days provide a unique opportunity to step back in time. These events often recreate moments from the past, offering insights into the people, challenges, and triumphs that shaped Route 66 and the communities along its path. They serve as a living museum, allowing travelers to interact with history in a tangible and engaging manner.

c. Community Connection:

Joining in these festivals allows travelers to connect deeply with local communities. It's during these gatherings that the true spirit of Route 66 shines brightest, as locals and visitors alike come together to celebrate, share stories, and create new memories. Such events are a testament to the enduring love and dedication locals have for preserving the legacy of Route 66.

d. Planning Around Events:

Given the diversity and allure of these festivals, it's beneficial to research the event calendar in advance. Aligning your trip with events that resonate with your interests can elevate your journey from a mere road trip to an unforgettable experience. Whether you're captivated by the roar of classic engines, the melodies of folk music, or tales from yesteryears, there's likely an event along Route 66 that will enrapture your heart.

In essence, the special events and festivals along Route 66 serve as bridges connecting travelers to the road's vibrant past and dynamic present. By immersing oneself in these celebrations, one can truly appreciate the depth of culture, community, and history that defines the unparalleled allure of Route 66.

- **4. Personal Preferences:**

When selecting the ideal time for your Route 66 adventure, it's essential to consider your own preferences and what kind of experience you envision. The timing of your journey should align with your unique tastes and desires, ensuring that your exploration of the Mother Road is tailored to your personal interests.

a. Vibrant Summer vs. Tranquil Shoulder Seasons:

Reflect on your affinity for different seasons and atmospheres. If you thrive in the vibrancy of summer with its bustling festivals and warm weather, planning a trip during this season can be invigorating. On the other hand, if you cherish tranquility and prefer a quieter ambiance, the shoulder seasons of spring or fall might better suit your temperament.

b. Weather Comfort:

Consider your comfort level with various weather conditions. Some travelers relish the heat of summer, while others prefer milder temperatures. If you're sensitive to extreme weather, you might opt for spring or fall when the climate is more moderate, allowing for a comfortable and enjoyable journey.

c. Festival and Event Alignment:

Take stock of your interests and hobbies. If you have a passion for classic cars, music, or history, research the Route 66 events and festivals that align with your preferences. Planning your trip around these gatherings can infuse your adventure with excitement and depth.

d. Time for Reflection:

Think about your personal goals for the trip. Do you seek a leisurely journey with ample time for reflection and exploration, or are you drawn to a more packed itinerary with numerous stops and activities? Tailoring the timing of your trip to your pace and preferences can significantly impact your overall satisfaction.

e. Budget Considerations:

Your budget also plays a role in determining the timing of your Route 66 adventure. Consider whether you can accommodate the potentially higher costs associated with peak tourist season or if you prefer to take advantage of offseason savings.

In essence, your Route 66 adventure is a personal odyssey, and your preferences should be at the forefront when choosing when to travel. Whether you thrive in bustling summer energy or seek the tranquility of a quieter season, Route 66 offers an experience that can be customized to your tastes and aspirations, ensuring that your journey along the Mother Road is an authentic reflection of your unique interests.

- **5. Road Conditions and Closures:**

While planning your Route 66 adventure, it's essential to be aware of the potential impact of road conditions and closures along the route. Route 66, like any highway, may undergo maintenance, repairs, or unexpected closures that can affect your journey. Staying informed and prepared can help you navigate these challenges effectively.

a. Routine Maintenance:

Roads, including Route 66, require routine maintenance to ensure safety and usability. Maintenance activities such as resurfacing, bridge repairs, or signage updates may result in temporary closures or detours. Be aware that these activities can impact your travel plans, so it's wise to check with local authorities or relevant agencies for information on scheduled maintenance.

b. Unforeseen Events:

Unforeseen events like weather-related incidents, accidents, or emergencies can also lead to road closures or detours. While you can't predict these occurrences, staying informed about current road conditions through local news sources or travel advisories can help you adjust your plans as needed.

c. Checking with Route 66 Associations:

Route 66 associations and preservation groups often have up-to-date information on the status of the highway and any road closures. These organizations are dedicated to keeping the spirit of Route 66 alive and can provide valuable insights into road conditions and alternative routes.

d. Planning for Delays:
As part of your travel preparation, it's advisable to build some flexibility into your itinerary to account for potential delays. This can help reduce stress and ensure that you have enough time to enjoy the sights and attractions along the way, even if you encounter road closures or detours.

e. Technology and Navigation:
Utilize modern navigation tools and apps that provide real-time updates on road conditions and traffic. GPS devices and smartphone apps can help you navigate around closures and find alternative routes as needed.

In summary, staying informed about road conditions and potential closures is a prudent step in planning your Route 66 adventure. While unexpected disruptions may occur, being prepared and adaptable will enable you to make the most of your journey and ensure a smoother and more enjoyable experience along the Mother Road.

- **6. Budget Considerations:**

Your budget is a fundamental aspect to weigh when determining the timing of your Route 66 adventure. The cost of your journey can fluctuate based on the time of year you choose to travel, so thoughtful financial planning is essential.

a. Peak Tourist Season Costs:
During the peak tourist season, typically in the summer months, Route 66 sees a surge in visitors. This increased demand can lead to higher prices for accommodations, dining, and activities. If you opt for a summer adventure, be prepared for potentially elevated costs and plan your budget accordingly.

b. Offseason Savings:
Traveling during the offseason, which often includes spring and fall, can offer cost-saving opportunities. Many accommodations and services may offer

discounted rates during these quieter periods to attract travelers. Lower demand can translate into more budget-friendly options for lodging and dining.

c. Midweek Advantage:

Weekdays, regardless of the season, typically see fewer tourists and lower prices than weekends. If you're looking to save on your Route 66 journey, consider scheduling your trip to include weekdays. You may find better deals on accommodations and have a more economical experience.

d. Balancing Costs and Experience:

While budget considerations are vital, it's also essential to strike a balance between costs and the experience you desire. Assess your priorities—whether you value a more budget-friendly journey or are willing to invest in a more vibrant summer adventure with higher expenses. Finding the right equilibrium ensures you have a fulfilling and financially manageable trip.

e. Planning and Reservations:

Regardless of the season you choose, it's wise to plan and book your accommodations and activities in advance. This not only helps secure better rates but also provides peace of mind, knowing that you have arrangements in place. Additionally, consider setting aside an emergency fund for unexpected expenses during your trip.

In conclusion, budget considerations play a significant role in deciding when to embark on your Route 66 adventure. While peak tourist season can be costlier, traveling during the offseason or midweek can offer savings opportunities. Balancing your budgetary goals with your travel aspirations will allow you to make the most of your journey along the Mother Road.

Pre-Trip Checklist

Before embarking on your Route 66 adventure, it's essential to ensure that you're well-prepared for the journey ahead. This pre-trip checklist will help you cover all the necessary details and make the most of your Mother Road experience:

Accommodation Reservations:

- Make reservations for accommodations along your route, especially during peak tourist season.

- Confirm your reservations closer to your travel date to avoid any surprises.

Vehicle Maintenance:

- Ensure your vehicle is in good working condition with regular maintenance, including oil changes, tire checks, and brake inspections.

- Carry a spare tire, jack, and essential tools for minor repairs.

Travel Documents:

- Check that you have all necessary travel documents, including identification, driver's license, and vehicle registration.

- If traveling internationally, ensure you have a valid passport and any required visas.

Travel Insurance:

- Consider purchasing travel insurance that covers unexpected events, such as trip cancellations, medical emergencies, or roadside assistance.

Packing Essentials:

- Prepare a packing list, including clothing suitable for the season and any specific activities or events you plan to attend.

- Pack essentials like toiletries, medications, chargers, and a first-aid kit.

Weather Preparedness:

- Check the weather forecast for your route and pack accordingly, including sunscreen, hats, rain gear, and cold-weather clothing if needed.

Emergency Kit:

- Assemble an emergency kit with items like a flashlight, batteries, a basic toolset, a fire extinguisher, and non-perishable snacks.

Travel Budget:

- Establish a budget for your trip, including daily expenses for food, accommodations, and activities.
- Carry cash and credit/debit cards for payment options along the route.

Reservations and Event Tickets:
- If planning to attend specific events or festivals, ensure you have purchased tickets or made reservations in advance.

Route 66 Association Information:
- Obtain contact information for local Route 66 associations or preservation groups. They can provide updates on road conditions and events.

Entertainment and Connectivity:
- Bring entertainment options for the road, such as music playlists, audiobooks, or travel games.
- Ensure your mobile devices are fully charged and have car chargers or power banks available.

Photography Gear:
- If you're a photography enthusiast, pack your camera, lenses, and accessories, along with extra memory cards and batteries.

Safety Precautions:
- Share your travel itinerary with a trusted friend or family member.
- Familiarize yourself with emergency contact numbers for the areas you'll be visiting.

Environmental Responsibility:
- Practice Leave No Trace principles by disposing of trash responsibly and respecting natural and cultural sites.

Local Cuisine and Dining Reservations:
- Research local cuisine along your route and plan to savor regional specialties.
- If there are specific restaurants you wish to visit, consider making reservations.

Expect the Unexpected:

   - Be open to detours and unexpected discoveries along the way. Some of the best Route 66 experiences happen off the beaten path.

By completing this pre-trip checklist, you'll be well-prepared to embark on your Route 66 adventure with confidence, ensuring a smooth and enjoyable journey along the Mother Road.

Budgeting for Your Journey

Budgeting for your Route 66 adventure is a crucial step in ensuring that you have a financially stress-free and enjoyable trip. Proper financial planning allows you to make the most of your journey while avoiding unexpected financial challenges. Here are essential steps to help you budget for your Route 66 adventure:

Set a Total Trip Budget:

   - Begin by determining the total amount you're willing to spend on your Route 66 adventure. This includes expenses such as accommodations, food, fuel, activities, and miscellaneous costs.

Break Down Your Expenses:

   - Create a detailed breakdown of your anticipated expenses. Consider categories such as lodging, dining, fuel, attractions, event tickets, and unexpected expenses.

Account for Special Events and Festivals:

   - If you plan to attend specific events or festivals along the route, include the cost of tickets, admission fees, and any related expenses in your budget.

Consider Seasonal Variations:

   - Take into account that costs may vary depending on the time of year you travel. Summer months and peak tourist season often come with higher prices for accommodations and activities.

Emergency Fund:

- Allocate a portion of your budget for emergencies or unexpected expenses. Having an emergency fund provides peace of mind and financial security during your journey.

Use a Travel Budgeting App:
  - Utilize travel budgeting apps or spreadsheet tools to track your expenses in real-time. These tools can help you stay within your budget and adjust spending as needed.

Daily Spending Limits:
  - Establish daily spending limits to help you manage your budget effectively. This can prevent overspending and ensure you stay on track.

Currency and Payment Methods:
  - Consider the currency and payment methods you'll use during your journey. Ensure you have access to cash and credit/debit cards that are widely accepted along the route.

Accommodation Reservations:
  - Make accommodation reservations in advance to secure favorable rates and avoid last-minute price surges.

Dining Choices:
  - Plan your dining choices, including both budget-friendly options and special dining experiences. Some of the best Route 66 experiences can be found in local diners and cafes.

Save on Fuel Costs:
  - Calculate estimated fuel costs based on your vehicle's fuel efficiency and the distance you'll be traveling. Consider fuel-saving driving habits to reduce expenses.

Cultural and Historical Sites:
  - Research admission fees for cultural and historical sites you plan to visit. Some may offer discounts for seniors, students, or military personnel.

Souvenirs and Shopping:
  - Allocate a portion of your budget for souvenirs and shopping. Remember that some unique finds along Route 66 can be excellent keepsakes.

Review and Adjust:
  - Periodically review your budget during the trip to ensure you're staying on track. If necessary, make adjustments to your spending plan to accommodate unexpected expenses or changes in your itinerary.

Enjoy the Journey:
  - While budgeting is essential, remember to savor the journey itself. Route 66 offers experiences that are often as valuable as any budget consideration.

By following these budgeting steps, you can embark on your Route 66 adventure with confidence, knowing that you have a solid financial plan in place. This allows you to focus on enjoying the iconic sights, experiences, and cultural treasures that the Mother Road has to offer.

Chapter 3: Navigating the Route

Navigating Route 66 is a journey through time and Americana, a road trip like no other. This historic highway, often referred to as the "Main Street of America," weaves through diverse landscapes, vibrant communities, and an ever-evolving cultural tapestry. As you embark on this iconic adventure, the art of navigation takes on new significance. It's not just about following road signs and GPS coordinates; it's about embracing the essence of exploration and discovery.

In this section, I'll guide you through the art of navigating Route 66, from understanding its historical significance to modern-day tools that make your journey smoother. We'll delve into the nuances of the road, highlighting must-visit attractions, hidden gems, and the stories that have shaped each mile. Whether you're an experienced road tripper or a first-time traveler, the road ahead promises a rich tapestry of experiences waiting to be uncovered. So, fasten your seatbelt, adjust your rearview mirror, and get ready to navigate the historic, scenic, and unforgettable Route 66.

GPS Coordinates and Navigation Tips

Certainly, navigating Route 66 can be a memorable adventure. Here are some GPS coordinates for key points along the route, along with navigation tips:

1. Chicago, Illinois (Starting Point):
    - GPS Coordinates: 41.8781° N, 87.6298° W
    - Navigation Tip: Begin your journey at Grant Park in Chicago, often marked by a Route 66 sign. Follow Jackson Boulevard westward.

2. St. Louis, Missouri:
    - GPS Coordinates (Gateway Arch): 38.6246° N, 90.1848° W
    - Navigation Tip: The iconic Gateway Arch in St. Louis marks a significant Route 66 stop. Explore the Arch grounds before continuing west.

3. Amarillo, Texas:
   - GPS Coordinates (Cadillac Ranch): 35.1874° N, 101.9877° W
   - Navigation Tip: Visit the unique Cadillac Ranch art installation just west of Amarillo for a quintessential Route 66 experience.

4. Winslow, Arizona:
   - GPS Coordinates (Standin' on the Corner Park): 35.0242° N, 110.6974° W
   - Navigation Tip: Don't miss the "Standin' on the Corner" Park, inspired by the Eagles' song, in Winslow.

5. Flagstaff, Arizona:
   - GPS Coordinates (Downtown Flagstaff): 35.1983° N, 111.6513° W
   - Navigation Tip: Explore the charming downtown area of Flagstaff and visit nearby attractions like the Meteor Crater.

6. Grand Canyon, Arizona (Detour):
   - GPS Coordinates (Grand Canyon Visitor Center): 36.0615° N, 112.1097° W
   - Navigation Tip: A detour to the Grand Canyon is highly recommended for its awe-inspiring beauty.

7. Los Angeles, California (Ending Point):
   - GPS Coordinates (Santa Monica Pier): 34.0085° N, 118.4977° W
   - Navigation Tip: Conclude your Route 66 journey at the iconic Santa Monica Pier in Los Angeles.

Navigation Tips:
- Use a GPS navigation system or a GPS app on your smartphone to follow Route 66. These tools can provide turn-by-turn directions and real-time updates on road conditions.

- Consider downloading offline maps for areas with limited cell service. This ensures you can navigate even in remote stretches of the route.

- Route 66 may have multiple alignments, so be prepared to follow signs and stay on the historic path. Research the specific alignments you want to explore.

- Embrace spontaneity and be open to detours and unexpected discoveries along the way. Some of the best Route 66 experiences happen when you venture off the main road.

- Pay attention to historic markers and roadside attractions. Route 66 is as much about the journey as the destination, and there are fascinating stories to uncover at every turn.

- Connect with local Route 66 associations and communities for insider tips and guidance on the best places to visit.

Remember that Route 66 is not just a road; it's an adventure through history, culture, and the American spirit. Enjoy the ride and create lasting memories along the Mother Road!

Mile-by-Mile Guide
Creating a mile-by-mile guide for a long and historically rich route like Route 66 is an extensive endeavor, and providing a detailed guide for the entire route here would be impractical. However, I can provide a simplified overview of some key points of interest along Route 66 mile by mile in different states. Keep in mind that Route 66 may have variations and different alignments, so it's essential to consult detailed Route 66 guidebooks or online resources for comprehensive guides.

Illinois:
- Mile 0: Chicago's Grant Park, the official starting point of Route 66.
- Mile 40: Joliet, known for its historic Route 66 attractions and the Route 66 Welcome Center.
- Mile 150: Springfield, the capital of Illinois and home to Abraham Lincoln's Presidential Library and Museum.

Missouri:

- Mile 291: St. Louis, where you can visit the iconic Gateway Arch and the Old Chain of Rocks Bridge.
- Mile 393: Cuba, famous for its murals and Wagon Wheel Motel.
- Mile 470: Springfield, another Springfield on Route 66, home to Route 66 Car Museum.

Oklahoma:
- Mile 431: Miami, Oklahoma, known for the Coleman Theater and Route 66 Vintage Iron Motorcycle Museum.
- Mile 449: Commerce, the hometown of Mickey Mantle, a baseball legend.
- Mile 440: Tulsa, a vibrant city with many Route 66 attractions and the Blue Whale.

Texas:
- Mile 571: Amarillo, where you can find the Cadillac Ranch and Big Texan Steak Ranch.
- Mile 650: Shamrock, with its iconic U-Drop Inn and Conoco Tower Station.
- Mile 729: McLean, home to the Devil's Rope Barbed Wire Museum.

New Mexico:
- Mile 815: Tucumcari, famous for its neon signs and historic motels.
- Mile 936: Albuquerque, New Mexico's largest city, offering cultural attractions and a scenic drive.
- Mile 1,113: Gallup, known for its Native American art and vibrant Route 66 vibe.

Arizona:
- Mile 1,377: Holbrook, featuring the historic Wigwam Motel and the Petrified Forest National Park.
- Mile 1,465: Winslow, where you can "Stand on the Corner" and explore Route 66 culture.
- Mile 1,577: Flagstaff, a gateway to the Grand Canyon and a hub for outdoor enthusiasts.

California:
- Mile 2,279: Needles, the last town in California before crossing into Arizona.

- Mile 2,342: Barstow, home to the Route 66 Mother Road Museum.
- Mile 2,448: Victorville, where you can visit the California Route 66 Museum.
- Mile 2,469: San Bernardino, known for its McDonald's Museum, often regarded as the first.

This is just a brief overview, and Route 66 offers numerous other attractions, landmarks, and unique experiences mile by mile. To plan a detailed journey along Route 66, consult dedicated Route 66 guidebooks and resources that provide comprehensive information on each segment of the route.

Chapter 4: Attractions and Landmarks

Iconic Stops and Must-See Attractions

Exploring Route 66 is a journey filled with iconic stops and must-see attractions that capture the essence of this historic highway. Here are some of the most renowned and unforgettable places to visit along the Mother Road:

Illinois:
1. Grant Park, Chicago (GPS Coordinates: 41.8781° N, 87.6298° W):

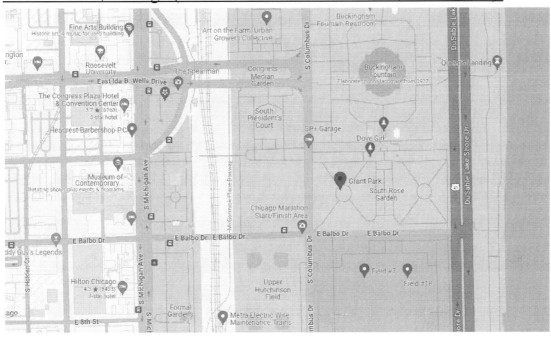

Your Route 66 journey commences at the iconic Grant Park in Chicago, often referred to as the "Front Yard of Chicago." This sprawling urban park is not only the starting point of the Mother Road but also a cultural hub with numerous attractions:

- Buckingham Fountain: Marvel at the grand Buckingham Fountain, one of the largest in the world, featuring captivating water displays and periodic light shows.

- Millennium Park: Stroll through Millennium Park and admire the famous "Bean" (Cloud Gate sculpture), the Jay Pritzker Pavilion, and Lurie Garden.

- Art Institute of Chicago: Explore the Art Institute of Chicago, home to an impressive collection of art, including famous works like Grant Wood's "American Gothic."

- Museum Campus: Visit the Museum Campus within Grant Park, housing renowned institutions like the Field Museum, the Shedd Aquarium, and the Adler Planetarium.

- Lakefront Trail: Enjoy a leisurely walk or bike ride along the scenic Lakefront Trail, which offers breathtaking views of Lake Michigan and the city skyline.

Grant Park serves as a vibrant cultural and recreational hub and provides an excellent starting point for your Route 66 adventure. From here, you'll set out on a journey that will take you through a diverse tapestry of landscapes, history, and culture as you follow the historic Route 66 signs westward. Soak in the energy of Chicago before embarking on your memorable road trip along the Mother Road.

2. Lou Mitchell's (GPS Coordinates: 41.8784° N, 87.6251° W):

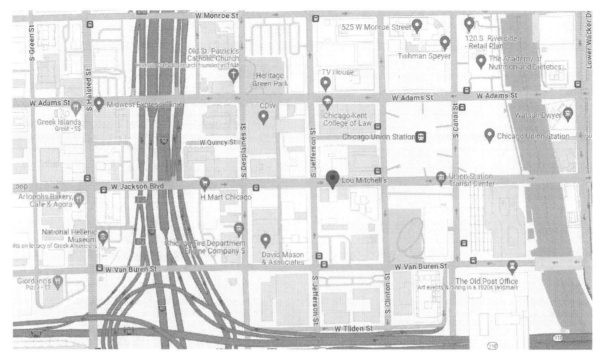

Located in the heart of Chicago, Lou Mitchell's is a legendary Route 66 diner that has been serving up delicious meals and a warm welcome to travelers since 1923. Here's why you should make a stop at this iconic eatery:

- Route 66 Tradition: Lou Mitchell's is a beloved Route 66 institution and a rite of passage for those beginning their journey along the Mother Road. As you step inside, you'll be greeted with a friendly "Welcome to Lou Mitchell's" and a complimentary donut hole—a tradition that's been upheld for decades.

- Hearty Breakfasts: The diner is renowned for its hearty breakfast offerings, including fluffy pancakes, omelets, corned beef hash, and homemade pies. It's the perfect place to fuel up for the road ahead.

- Vintage Atmosphere: Lou Mitchell's retains its vintage charm with classic diner decor, neon signs, and an old-school counter where you can watch the skilled chefs at work.

- Friendly Service: The staff at Lou Mitchell's is known for their warm hospitality and attentive service, making you feel like a cherished guest.

- Route 66 Memorabilia: The walls are adorned with Route 66 memorabilia, adding to the nostalgic ambiance and providing a glimpse into the history of the iconic highway.

Before embarking on your Route 66 adventure, a visit to Lou Mitchell's is a must. It's not just a meal but an experience that connects you to the tradition and spirit of the Mother Road. Enjoy a hearty breakfast, soak in the vintage atmosphere, and collect memories that will stay with you throughout your journey.

3. Route 66 Hall of Fame and Museum (Pontiac, Illinois - GPS Coordinates: 40.8806° N, 88.6274° W):

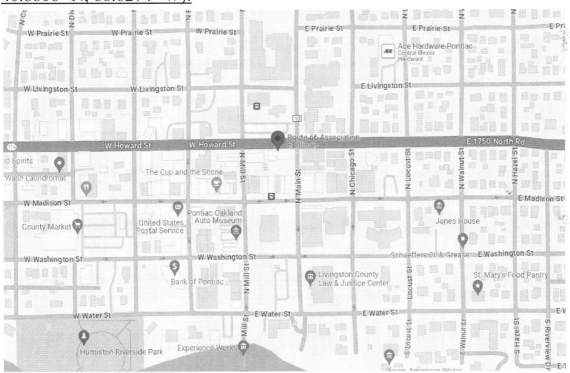

Nestled in the heart of Pontiac, Illinois, the Route 66 Hall of Fame and Museum is a treasure trove of history and nostalgia dedicated to the iconic Mother Road. Here's what you can anticipate during your visit:

- Immersive Route 66 History: Step back in time and immerse yourself in the rich history of Route 66. The museum's exhibits, memorabilia, and narratives provide an in-depth look at the evolution and cultural significance of this historic highway.

- Vintage Automobiles: Marvel at a remarkable collection of vintage cars and vehicles that once journeyed along Route 66. These well-preserved automobiles offer a glimpse into the golden age of American road trips.

- Route 66 Memorabilia: Explore an extensive array of Route 66 memorabilia, including signs, postcards, and artifacts that encapsulate the unique culture and Americana associated with the highway.

- Hall of Fame Tribute: Pay homage to the trailblazers and individuals who have made exceptional contributions to the preservation and celebration of Route 66. The Hall of Fame section honors those who have played a pivotal role in keeping the spirit of the road alive.

- Interactive Exhibits: Engage with interactive exhibits that allow you to delve deeper into the history and ethos of Route 66. Learn about the diverse array of people, places, and stories that have left their mark on this iconic highway.

- Gift Shop: Don't forget to peruse the museum's gift shop, where you can find an array of Route 66-themed souvenirs, books, and memorabilia to commemorate your visit.

The Route 66 Hall of Fame and Museum in Pontiac, Illinois, is a must-visit destination for anyone embarking on a journey along the Mother Road. It offers a captivating exploration of the past and present of Route 66, shedding light on its enduring legacy and its profound impact on American culture and history.

Missouri:
4. Gateway Arch, St. Louis (GPS Coordinates: 38.6246° N, 90.1848° W):

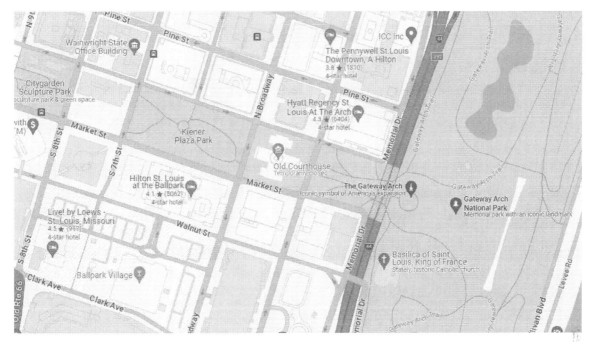

The Gateway Arch in St. Louis, Missouri, is an architectural masterpiece and a symbol of westward expansion in the United States. Here's why it's a must-visit stop along your Route 66 journey:

- Iconic Symbol: The Gateway Arch is one of America's most recognized symbols. It stands at 630 feet (192 meters) tall and serves as a tribute to the westward expansion of the United States during the 19th century.

- Architectural Marvel: Designed by renowned architect Eero Saarinen, the stainless steel arch is a marvel of modern architecture. Its sleek and graceful curves are a sight to behold.

- Tram Ride: Take a tram ride to the top of the arch for breathtaking panoramic views of the Mississippi River, downtown St. Louis, and the surrounding area. The tram ride is an unforgettable experience.

- Museum and Visitor Center: Explore the Museum of Westward Expansion located beneath the arch. It provides a comprehensive look at the history of westward expansion, including Lewis and Clark's expedition.

- Riverfront Park: The grounds around the Gateway Arch offer a beautiful riverfront park where you can relax, take a stroll, and appreciate the serene beauty of the Mississippi River.

- Gateway Arch Riverboat Cruises: Consider taking a riverboat cruise on the Mississippi River to complement your visit to the arch.

The Gateway Arch is not only a remarkable monument but also a symbol of America's pioneering spirit and the historic westward journey. It's a testament to the adventurous spirit that Route 66 travelers have embodied for generations. Be sure to set aside time to marvel at this iconic landmark when passing through St. Louis on your Route 66 adventure.

5. Meramec Caverns (GPS Coordinates: 38.2769° N, 91.0805° W):

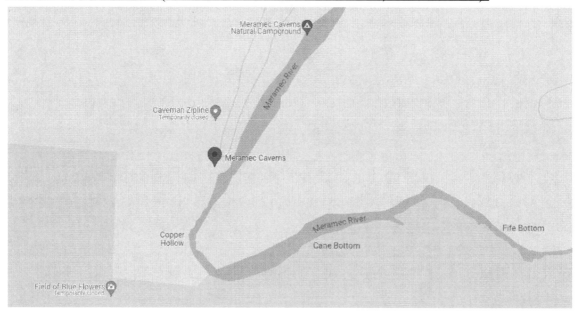

Located near Stanton, Missouri, Meramec Caverns is a captivating natural wonder and a memorable stop along Route 66. Here's why you should consider exploring the fascinating underground world of Meramec Caverns:

- Spectacular Caves: Meramec Caverns is known for its breathtaking limestone caves that extend for miles beneath the surface. Guided tours take you through this subterranean wonderland, where you'll encounter stunning formations, stalactites, stalagmites, and underground rivers.

- Jesse James Hideout: The caverns have a historical connection to the infamous outlaw Jesse James. It's believed that he and his gang used the caves as a hideout, adding a layer of intrigue to the site.

- Cavern Lighting: The caverns are beautifully illuminated, showcasing the natural beauty of the rock formations. The play of light and shadow adds to the enchantment of the underground experience.

- Cave Restaurant and Souvenirs: Above ground, you'll find amenities such as a cave-themed restaurant and gift shop where you can purchase souvenirs to remember your visit.

- Scenic Picnic Area: Meramec Caverns offers a scenic picnic area surrounded by lush greenery, making it an ideal spot for a leisurely break and enjoying the natural surroundings.

Exploring Meramec Caverns allows you to venture beneath the Earth's surface and witness the awe-inspiring geological formations that have been thousands of years in the making. It's a unique and memorable addition to your Route 66 journey, providing a contrast to the above-ground adventures along the Mother Road. Don't forget to bring your camera to capture the stunning underground landscapes.

6. Chain of Rocks Bridge (GPS Coordinates: 38.7484° N, 90.1892° W):

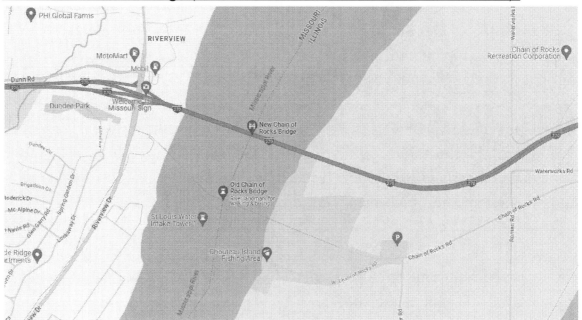

The Chain of Rocks Bridge, situated near St. Louis, Missouri, is a historic and iconic Route 66 crossing that offers a unique experience for travelers. Here's why it's worth a visit:

- Historic Crossing: The Chain of Rocks Bridge is a historic bridge that once served as a crucial river crossing along Route 66. It spans the mighty Mississippi River, connecting Missouri to Illinois.

- Distinctive Design: What sets this bridge apart is its unique 22-degree bend in the middle, giving it a distinctive appearance and the "Chain of Rocks" name. The bend was designed to accommodate riverboat traffic.

- Scenic Walk or Cycle: Today, the bridge is a pedestrian and cycling bridge, allowing visitors to stroll or bike across the Mississippi River. It provides an excellent opportunity to enjoy the scenic beauty of the river and capture stunning photos of the surroundings.

- Mississippi River Views: As you make your way across the Chain of Rocks Bridge, you'll be treated to fantastic views of the Mississippi River, which has played a significant role in American history and culture.

- Historic Route 66 Ambiance: The bridge retains its historic Route 66 ambiance, and walking or cycling across it allows you to step back in time and connect with the road's rich heritage.

Visiting the Chain of Rocks Bridge is a memorable way to experience the legacy of Route 66 while taking in the natural beauty and history of the Mississippi River. Whether you're a history enthusiast, a cyclist, or simply seeking picturesque views, this bridge has something to offer every traveler on the Mother Road.

Oklahoma:
7. Blue Whale, Catoosa, Oklahoma (GPS Coordinates: 36.1896° N, 95.7425° W):

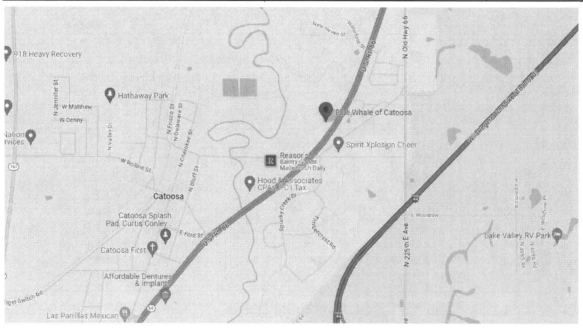

The Blue Whale in Catoosa, Oklahoma, is a whimsical and iconic Route 66 attraction that promises a unique and playful stop. Here's why you should plan to snap a photo with this beloved roadside giant:

- Iconic Roadside Attraction: The Blue Whale is a quintessential example of the quirky and charming roadside attractions that dot Route 66. This smiling blue behemoth has become an enduring symbol of the Mother Road.

- Swimming Hole: Originally built as a family swimming hole in the 1970s, the Blue Whale provided a refreshing oasis for travelers and locals alike. While swimming is no longer allowed, the whale's significance as a historic landmark remains.

- Photo Opportunity: The Blue Whale offers an irresistible photo opportunity. Pose alongside this cheerful and oversized aquatic creature, capturing a whimsical memory of your Route 66 journey.

- Picnic Area: The site surrounding the Blue Whale features a picnic area where you can relax, have a snack, or simply enjoy the surroundings. It's an ideal spot for a brief respite on your road trip.

- Nostalgic Appeal: The Blue Whale represents the nostalgia and creativity of Route 66's heyday when imaginative attractions were designed to delight and surprise travelers.

Visiting the Blue Whale is not only a chance to take a memorable photograph but also an opportunity to connect with the sense of wonder and playfulness that Route 66 embodies. This whimsical attraction is a delightful reminder of the spirit of exploration that defines the Mother Road.

8. Round Barn, Arcadia, Oklahoma (GPS Coordinates: 35.6463° N, 97.3315° W):

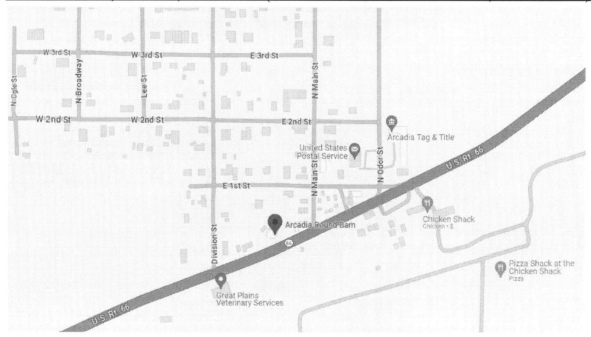

The Round Barn in Arcadia, Oklahoma, is a charming and historic landmark along Route 66 that showcases unique architecture and a slice of American nostalgia. Here's why you should plan a visit to this iconic site:

- Architectural Wonder: The Round Barn is a one-of-a-kind architectural gem. It's a fully restored round barn that harkens back to a bygone era when such structures were not uncommon but have since become rare.

- Unusual Design: The barn's circular design is unusual and eye-catching, making it a distinctive and memorable stop on your Route 66 journey. The craftsmanship and attention to detail in its construction are impressive.

- Visitor Center: Inside the Round Barn, you'll find a visitor center that provides insights into the history of the barn, Route 66, and the surrounding area. Friendly volunteers are often on hand to answer questions and share stories.

- Gift Shop: Browse the on-site gift shop for Route 66 souvenirs, local crafts, and unique mementos to commemorate your visit.

- Photo Opportunities: The Round Barn offers excellent photo opportunities both inside and outside the barn. Capture its unique architecture and the nostalgic atmosphere of this historic site.

- Picnic Area: The surrounding grounds include a picnic area, allowing you to relax, enjoy a meal, and soak in the peaceful countryside ambiance.

Visiting the Round Barn in Arcadia is a delightful way to experience the quirks and charms of Route 66. It's a testament to the road's ability to preserve and celebrate unique landmarks that capture the essence of American road tripping. Don't miss the opportunity to explore this architectural treasure along your Route 66 adventure.

Texas:
9. Cadillac Ranch, Amarillo, Texas (GPS Coordinates: 35.1874° N, 101.9873° W):

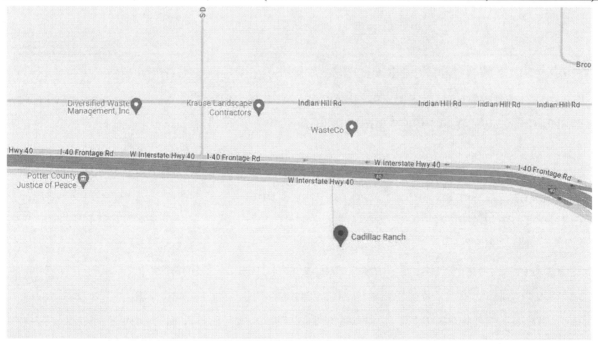

Cadillac Ranch is a whimsical and iconic art installation that stands as a must-see stop on your Route 66 adventure. Here's why you should experience this unique attraction:

- Artistic Marvel: Cadillac Ranch is not your typical roadside attraction. It's an art installation consisting of ten Cadillacs buried nose-down in a field. The cars are partially submerged in the ground at the same angle as the Great Pyramid of Giza, creating a visually striking and surreal landscape.

- Interactive Art: One of the most captivating aspects of Cadillac Ranch is that visitors are encouraged to participate in the art. Bring along a can of spray paint and leave your mark on the Cadillacs. Over the years, these cars have been covered in layers of colorful graffiti, creating a constantly evolving and vibrant work of art.

- Cultural Icon: Cadillac Ranch has become a symbol of Route 66 and American pop culture. It embodies the spirit of freedom and creativity that the road represents.

- Photo Opportunities: Capture memorable photos of yourself amidst the spray-painted Cadillacs, or take a shot of the colorful cars against the expansive Texas sky.

- Visitor-Friendly: Cadillac Ranch is easily accessible, located just off Route 66 near Amarillo. It's a short walk from the road, making it convenient for travelers.

- Nostalgic Vibe: The combination of vintage cars, pop art, and the open Texas landscape creates a nostalgic and captivating atmosphere.

Experiencing Cadillac Ranch is not just about viewing art; it's about participating in it. Leave your mark on this ever-changing canvas, and be part of the creative legacy that has been going strong since the 1970s. It's an iconic stop that perfectly embodies the spirit of Route 66's roadside wonders.

10. Palo Duro Canyon State Park, Texas (GPS Coordinates: 34.9196° N, 101.6737° W):

Often referred to as the "Grand Canyon of Texas," Palo Duro Canyon State Park is a natural wonder that beckons travelers with its breathtaking beauty. Here's why you should make time to explore this stunning destination along your Route 66 journey:

- Spectacular Scenery: Palo Duro Canyon is the second-largest canyon in the United States and offers a dramatic landscape of towering red rock formations, rugged cliffs, and sweeping vistas. The colors and geological features of the canyon are a photographer's dream.

- Outdoor Adventures: The park provides numerous opportunities for outdoor activities such as hiking, mountain biking, horseback riding, and birdwatching. There are trails suitable for all skill levels, from leisurely walks to challenging hikes.

- Scenic Drives: If you prefer to take in the sights from the comfort of your vehicle, the park offers scenic drives that provide panoramic views of the canyon.

- Historical Significance: Palo Duro Canyon has historical significance, as it was once home to Native American tribes and served as a location in the Red River War of the 1870s.

- Visitor Center: Stop by the visitor center to learn about the park's history, geology, and wildlife. The knowledgeable park rangers can provide guidance and information.

- Camping and Picnicking: Palo Duro Canyon State Park offers camping facilities, picnic areas, and even a musical drama performance called "TEXAS," which tells the story of the Texas Panhandle.

Visiting Palo Duro Canyon allows you to connect with the natural beauty of Texas and appreciate the diverse landscapes that Route 66 traverses. Whether you're an outdoor enthusiast, a nature lover, or simply seeking awe-inspiring scenery, this state park provides a memorable experience that showcases the grandeur of the American Southwest.

11. The Big Texan Steak Ranch, Amarillo, Texas (GPS Coordinates: 35.1885° N, 101.8086° W):

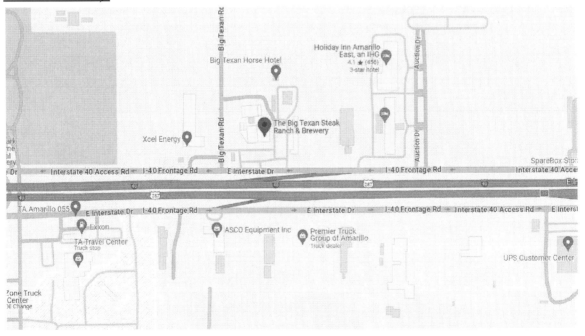

The Big Texan Steak Ranch is not just a restaurant; it's an iconic Texas experience along Route 66. Here's why you should consider dining at this legendary establishment:

- The 72-Ounce Steak Challenge: The Big Texan is famous for its daring "72-Ounce Steak Challenge." If you're up for it, you can attempt to eat a massive 72-ounce (4.5-pound) steak, along with a baked potato, shrimp cocktail, salad, and a bread roll within a set time limit. Successfully completing the challenge not only earns you a free meal but also a coveted spot in the restaurant's Hall of Fame.

- Authentic Texas Dining: Whether you take on the challenge or opt for a more traditional meal, The Big Texan serves up delicious and hearty Texan fare, including steaks, ribs, burgers, and more.

- Texas Hospitality: The restaurant exudes warm and welcoming Texas hospitality, providing a memorable dining experience for travelers. The staff is known for their friendliness and entertaining flair.

- Western Atmosphere: The Big Texan embraces a Western atmosphere with cowboy decor, neon signs, and a rustic charm that captures the spirit of the American Southwest.

- Gift Shop: Explore the on-site gift shop, where you can find souvenirs and unique items to commemorate your visit.

- Live Music: Enjoy live music in the bar area on select evenings, adding to the festive ambiance.

Dining at The Big Texan Steak Ranch is not just about enjoying a delicious meal; it's about immersing yourself in Texas culture, cuisine, and hospitality. Whether you're a steak enthusiast or simply seeking a taste of the Lone Star State, this iconic restaurant is a memorable stop on your Route 66 journey. And if you're feeling adventurous, the steak challenge might be your chance for glory.

New Mexico:
12. Blue Hole, Santa Rosa, New Mexico (GPS Coordinates: 34.9420° N, 104.6614° W):

The Blue Hole in Santa Rosa is a natural oasis and an inviting stop along Route 66. Here's why you should consider taking a refreshing dip in its crystal-clear waters:

- Natural Wonder: The Blue Hole is a unique geological formation, often referred to as a "cenote." It's a natural sinkhole filled with incredibly clear and blue water.

The depth of the water is around 81 feet (25 meters), making it a popular spot for scuba diving and swimming.

- Swimming Paradise: If you're seeking respite from the road and the heat, the Blue Hole provides a perfect opportunity to cool off. The water is cool, clear, and inviting, making it a popular spot for swimmers and snorkelers.

- Scuba Diving: The Blue Hole is renowned in the scuba diving community for its excellent visibility and the chance to explore underwater caves and formations. If you're a certified diver, you can take the plunge and explore the depths.

- Picnic Area: The surrounding area offers picnic tables and shaded spots, providing a pleasant setting for a leisurely meal or relaxation.

- Scenic Setting: The vivid blue waters of the Blue Hole contrast beautifully with the desert landscape, creating a striking and picturesque setting.

- Local Attraction: Santa Rosa embraces the Blue Hole as a local attraction and takes pride in its natural beauty. The site is well-maintained and easily accessible from Route 66.

Taking a dip in the Blue Hole is a refreshing and invigorating experience that adds a natural element to your Route 66 adventure. Whether you're a swimmer, a diver, or simply looking to enjoy the tranquility of this natural wonder, the Blue Hole in Santa Rosa offers a unique and memorable stop along the Mother Road.

Arizona:
13. Wigwam Motel, Holbrook, Arizona (GPS Coordinates: 34.9014° N, 110.1634° W):

Spending a night at the Wigwam Motel in Holbrook is a truly unique and nostalgic experience along Route 66. Here's why you should consider staying in one of the iconic wigwam-shaped motel rooms:

- Iconic Accommodation: The Wigwam Motel is known for its distinctive and charming wigwam-shaped rooms. These concrete teepees are a throwback to the roadside motels of yesteryear and have become an enduring symbol of Route 66.

- Nostalgic Atmosphere: The motel exudes a nostalgic atmosphere that takes you back to the golden age of American road trips. It's a step back in time to an era when travelers sought adventure and comfort along Route 66.

- Comfortable Lodging: Despite their unique shape, the wigwam rooms offer comfortable and modern amenities, including cozy beds, private bathrooms, and air conditioning. You'll have a comfortable night's rest while enjoying the novelty of your surroundings.

- Photo Opportunities: The Wigwam Motel is a prime spot for capturing memorable photos. The teepees lit up at night create a whimsical and enchanting scene.

- Friendly Staff: The staff at the Wigwam Motel are known for their friendliness and hospitality, adding to the welcoming ambiance.

- Historic Significance: The Wigwam Motel is listed on the National Register of Historic Places, highlighting its importance in preserving the history of Route 66.

Spending a night in a wigwam at the Wigwam Motel is not just about lodging; it's about immersing yourself in the history and ambiance of Route 66. It's a chance to create lasting memories and be part of the rich tapestry of the Mother Road's heritage. Whether you're an architecture enthusiast, a history buff, or simply seeking a unique overnight stay, the Wigwam Motel in Holbrook is a must-experience destination on your Route 66 journey.

14. Petrified Forest National Park, Arizona (GPS Coordinates: 34.9091° N, 109.8068° W):

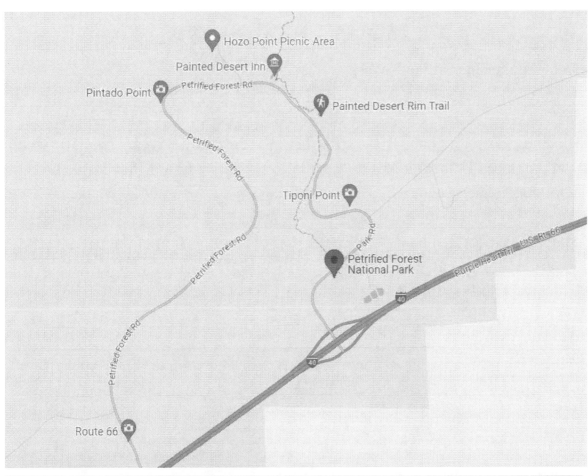

Petrified Forest National Park is a remarkable and geologically rich destination along Route 66. Here's why you should make time to witness the colorful petrified wood and unique desert landscapes:

- Petrified Wood: The park is renowned for its vast deposits of petrified wood, which date back to the Late Triassic Period, over 200 million years ago. The wood has undergone a fascinating process of fossilization, resulting in beautiful and colorful crystalline structures.

- Scenic Drives: Route 66 passes through the southern portion of the park, providing an opportunity for a scenic drive. The park's main road, known as the "Painted Desert Rim Drive," offers stunning vistas of the Painted Desert and access to key points of interest.

- Hiking Trails: Petrified Forest National Park features several hiking trails of varying lengths and difficulty levels. These trails lead you through the park's unique landscapes and offer the chance to see petroglyphs, ancient ruins, and, of course, petrified wood up close.

- Painted Desert: The park encompasses a portion of the Painted Desert, a mesmerizing landscape of colorful badlands, mesas, and buttes. The ever-changing colors of the desert provide a captivating sight, especially during sunrise and sunset.

- Visitor Centers: The park has two visitor centers, the Painted Desert Visitor Center and the Rainbow Forest Museum. Both offer educational exhibits, interpretive programs, and information to enhance your understanding of the park's geology, paleontology, and cultural history.

- Photography: Petrified Forest National Park is a photographer's paradise. The unique landscapes, the vibrant colors of the petrified wood, and the stark beauty of the desert make for excellent photographic opportunities.

Visiting Petrified Forest National Park is a journey through time and a chance to explore ancient landscapes that have been preserved for millennia. It's an opportunity to connect with the geological wonders of the American Southwest and appreciate the natural beauty that Route 66 has to offer. Whether you're a nature enthusiast, a history buff, or an art lover, this park has something to captivate every traveler.

15. Grand Canyon National Park, Arizona (GPS Coordinates: 36.1069° N, 112.1129° W):

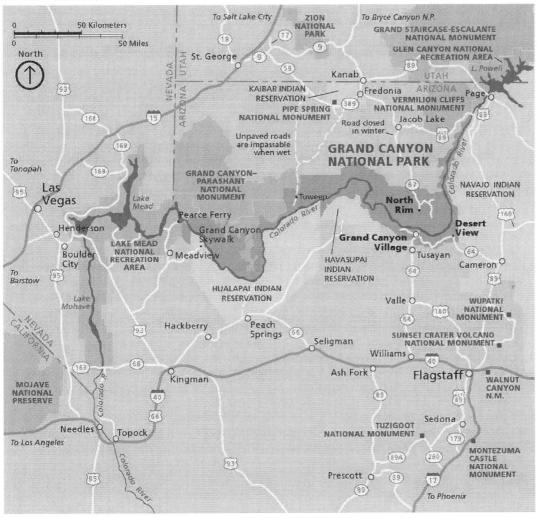

While not directly on Route 66, the Grand Canyon is a magnificent natural wonder that's worth a detour. Here's why you should consider experiencing the awe-inspiring beauty of one of the world's most famous national parks:

- Natural Wonder: The Grand Canyon is often described as one of Earth's most breathtaking natural wonders. Its immense size, depth, and colorful rock formations leave visitors in awe of the power of nature. Standing on the rim and gazing into the canyon is a humbling and unforgettable experience.

- Spectacular Views: The park offers numerous viewpoints along the rim, each providing a different perspective of the canyon's vastness and geological diversity. Sunrise and sunset at the Grand Canyon are particularly magical, as the changing light creates a canvas of colors.

- Hiking and Exploration: For those who want to venture into the canyon, there are hiking trails that lead to the Colorado River below. While some trails are challenging, others offer more accessible options for visitors of varying fitness levels.

- Visitor Centers: The Grand Canyon has multiple visitor centers that provide information, maps, and educational exhibits to help you make the most of your visit. Park rangers are available to answer questions and offer guidance.

- Cultural Heritage: The Grand Canyon is also home to a rich cultural heritage, with historical sites and the legacy of Native American tribes that have inhabited the area for centuries.

- Scenic Drives: The drive through the park offers stunning views even if you choose not to hike. The Desert View Drive, for example, provides a scenic route along the canyon's rim.

Visiting the Grand Canyon is a once-in-a-lifetime experience that allows you to connect with the grandeur of nature and appreciate the vastness of our planet. While it's a detour from Route 66, it's a detour that promises to be one of the highlights of your journey. Whether you're a nature lover, an adventurer, or simply someone seeking inspiration from the natural world, the Grand Canyon delivers an unforgettable experience.

California:
16. Santa Monica Pier, Los Angeles, California (GPS Coordinates: 34.0082° N, 118.4976° W):

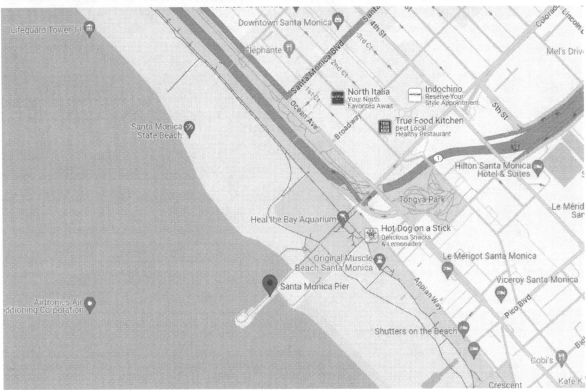

Concluding your Route 66 journey at the Santa Monica Pier in Los Angeles is a fitting and picturesque end to your adventure. Here's why you should choose this iconic location as the finale of your trip:

- Historic Endpoint: The Santa Monica Pier serves as the symbolic endpoint of Route 66. It's where the Mother Road officially meets the Pacific Ocean, marking the completion of your cross-country journey.

- Scenic Beauty: The pier offers stunning views of the Pacific Ocean and the California coastline. The combination of sun, sea, and sand creates a picturesque backdrop for reflection and celebration.

- Amusement Park: The pier features Pacific Park, a seaside amusement park with a Ferris wheel, roller coaster, and other rides. It's a fun and vibrant place to enjoy some leisure time and savor the coastal atmosphere.

- Shopping and Dining: Explore the shops and restaurants along the pier and nearby Third Street Promenade, where you can find a variety of cuisines, souvenirs, and unique items.

- Beach Access: The pier is adjacent to Santa Monica Beach, offering a chance to dip your toes in the Pacific Ocean or take a leisurely stroll along the sandy shores.

- Entertainment: The pier often hosts live music, performances, and events, creating a lively and festive atmosphere.

- Iconic Photo Op: Don't forget to capture a photo at the "End of the Trail" sign, which marks the terminus of Route 66 and celebrates your cross-country journey.

Concluding your Route 66 adventure at Santa Monica Pier is a momentous and memorable experience. It's a chance to celebrate your journey, reflect on the miles traveled, and take in the beauty of the Pacific Coast. Whether you're traveling with friends, family, or on your own, it's a destination that embodies the spirit of accomplishment and the joy of exploration.

17. Joshua Tree National Park, California (GPS Coordinates: 33.8734° N, 115.9006° W):

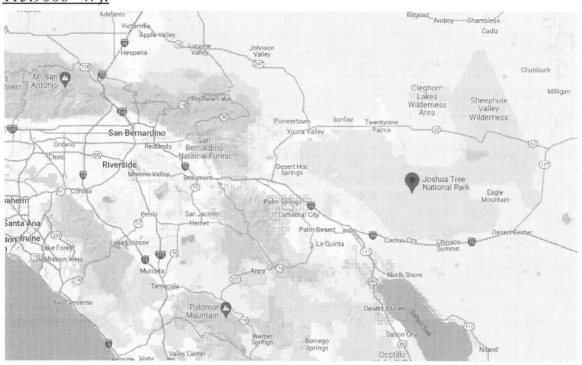

While not directly on Route 66, Joshua Tree National Park is a captivating destination that's well worth a detour. Here's why you should consider exploring the surreal landscapes of this unique park:

- Otherworldly Scenery: Joshua Tree National Park is renowned for its otherworldly landscapes, characterized by towering Joshua Trees, rugged rock formations, and a desert environment that feels like something out of a science fiction movie.

- Rock Climbing: The park is a haven for rock climbers, with its distinctive rock formations providing a challenging and scenic playground for climbers of all skill levels.

- Hiking Trails: Joshua Tree offers a variety of hiking trails, ranging from short walks to longer treks. Each trail showcases different aspects of the park's geology, flora, and fauna.

- Stargazing: The park's remote location and low light pollution make it an excellent place for stargazing. On clear nights, the desert sky is a canvas of stars, planets, and celestial wonders.

- Wildlife Viewing: Keep an eye out for desert wildlife, including bighorn sheep, coyotes, and a variety of bird species. The park's unique ecosystems support a surprising diversity of creatures.

- Photography Opportunities: Whether you're an amateur or professional photographer, Joshua Tree offers endless opportunities for capturing the stark beauty and surreal landscapes of the desert.

- Visitor Centers: The park has visitor centers that provide information, maps, and exhibits about the park's geology, ecology, and cultural history.

Detouring to Joshua Tree National Park is an opportunity to immerse yourself in the stark and mesmerizing beauty of the California desert. It's a destination that appeals to nature lovers, outdoor enthusiasts, photographers, and anyone seeking a unique and unforgettable experience. While it may be a slight deviation from Route 66, it promises to be a detour you'll cherish.

18.The Hollywood Sign and Walk of Fame, Los Angeles, California (GPS Coordinates: 34.1341° N, 118.3215° W):

Exploring the iconic Hollywood Sign and the Walk of Fame in Los Angeles is a chance to immerse yourself in the glitz and glamour of the entertainment industry. Here's why you should consider adding these famous attractions to your Route 66 journey:

- Hollywood Sign: The Hollywood Sign is one of the most recognizable symbols of the entertainment world. Viewing this colossal sign perched in the Hollywood Hills is an opportunity to appreciate the history and allure of the movie-making capital.

- Hiking: For a closer encounter with the sign, consider taking a hike to the Griffith Observatory, which offers panoramic views of Los Angeles and a chance to see the sign up close.

- Walk of Fame: The Hollywood Walk of Fame is a sidewalk embedded with more than 2,600 brass stars bearing the names of famous entertainers from the worlds of film, television, music, and theater. Strolling along the Walk of Fame allows you to discover the names of your favorite stars and pay homage to entertainment legends.

- Grauman's Chinese Theatre: Nearby, you'll find Grauman's Chinese Theatre, famous for its historic movie premieres and its forecourt with imprints of celebrities' hand and footprints.

- Entertainment and Dining: Hollywood offers a wealth of entertainment options, including theaters, live performances, and restaurants. It's a place to savor the nightlife and the vibrant energy of Tinseltown.

- Shopping: Hollywood is also home to a variety of shops and boutiques, making it a great place to indulge in some retail therapy and pick up souvenirs.

Visiting the Hollywood Sign and the Walk of Fame is a chance to step into the world of show business and explore the heart of the entertainment industry. It's a detour from Route 66 that brings you face to face with the legends, glitz, and history of Hollywood, providing a memorable and star-studded experience along your journey.

These are just a few of the many iconic stops and must-see attractions along Route 66. Each stretch of the route offers its own unique charm, history, and cultural treasures, making Route 66 a road trip like no other. Be sure to consult Route 66 guidebooks and resources for more in-depth information on these and other remarkable places along the way.

Hidden Gems Along the Route

Exploring hidden gems along Route 66 is a rewarding part of the journey, as they often offer unique and lesser-known experiences. Here are some hidden gems to consider adding to your Route 66 adventure:

1. El Morro National Monument, New Mexico:

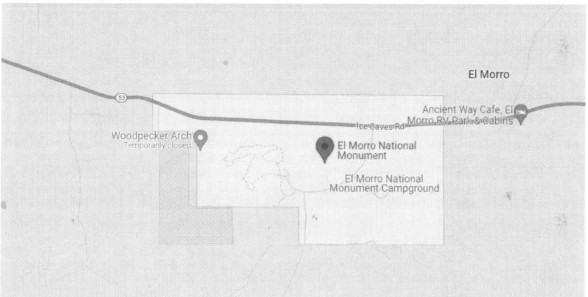

A detour to El Morro National Monument is like stepping into a time capsule that combines natural beauty, history, and cultural significance. Here's why this hidden gem is a must-visit for history and nature enthusiasts:

- Ancient Petroglyphs: El Morro, also known as "Inscription Rock," features a remarkable collection of ancient petroglyphs etched into the sandstone cliffs. These petroglyphs, created by Native Americans centuries ago, offer a glimpse into the spiritual and artistic expressions of the past.

- Historical Inscriptions: As you explore the base of the sandstone bluff, you'll encounter inscriptions left by early travelers, including Spanish explorers,

American pioneers, and Native Americans. These inscriptions tell stories of journeys, encounters, and survival in the harsh desert landscape.

- Waterhole Oasis: At the base of El Morro, you'll discover a natural water pool, a rare find in the arid Southwest. This oasis was a crucial stopping point for travelers throughout history, providing a vital water source for both humans and animals.

- Hiking Trails: El Morro offers several hiking trails that lead you through the park, allowing you to appreciate both the natural and historical aspects of the monument. The Headland Trail takes you to the top of the sandstone bluff, offering breathtaking panoramic views of the surrounding desert.

- Visitor Center: The visitor center at El Morro provides valuable information about the monument's history, geology, and significance. Park rangers are available to answer questions and enhance your understanding of the site.

- Cultural Heritage: El Morro National Monument is a testament to the diverse cultural heritage of the American Southwest. It's a place where Native American, Spanish, and American histories intersect and coexist.

- Scenic Beauty: The rugged beauty of El Morro, with its towering sandstone cliffs and desert landscapes, provides a stunning backdrop for exploration and photography.

Visiting El Morro National Monument is a chance to connect with the ancient traditions of Native Americans, the exploratory spirit of early travelers, and the unique geological features of the region. It's a hidden gem that offers a blend of natural wonder and cultural significance, making it a fascinating stop along your Route 66 journey.

2. Sandhills Curiosity Shop, Erick, Oklahoma:

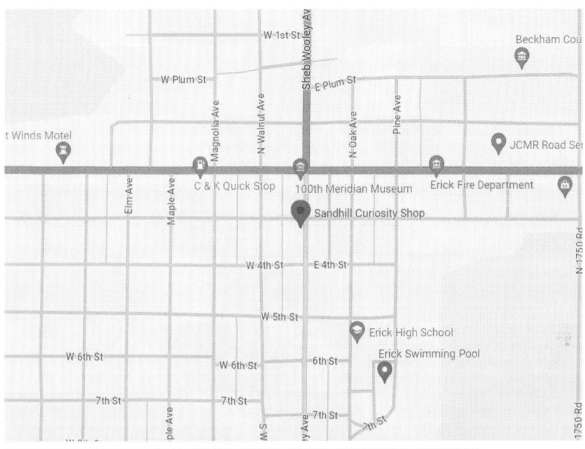

If you're in search of an offbeat and charming attraction that embodies the quirky spirit of Route 66, the Sandhills Curiosity Shop in Erick, Oklahoma, is a hidden gem that promises a one-of-a-kind experience. Here's why you should make a detour to visit this eclectic and captivating place:

- Musical Talents: Harley and Annabelle Russell, the proprietors of the Sandhills Curiosity Shop, are not only collectors but also talented musicians. Their impromptu musical performances are a delightful addition to your visit. You might find yourself tapping your feet to the tunes of the Mother Road.

- Eclectic Collections: The shop is a treasure trove of memorabilia, antiques, and oddities that the Russells have collected over the years. From vintage signs and quirky artifacts to antique motorcycles and Route 66-themed items, there's no shortage of fascinating things to explore.

- Personal Connection: The Russells are known for their warmth and hospitality. They often engage with visitors, sharing stories of their own Route 66 adventures and offering insights into the hidden treasures and legends of the road.

- Photo Opportunities: The Sandhills Curiosity Shop is a photographer's dream. The unique and eccentric displays provide ample opportunities for memorable photographs. Don't forget to capture the essence of Route 66 and the Russells' creativity.

- Authentic Route 66 Vibe: This attraction embodies the authenticity and character of Route 66. It's not a corporate tourist destination but a labor of love by passionate individuals who want to share the spirit of the Mother Road with fellow travelers.

- Supporting Local Business: Visiting the Sandhills Curiosity Shop is a chance to support a local, family-owned business that adds to the charm and character of Route 66. Your patronage contributes to the preservation of the road's unique culture.

- Hidden Treasures: Erick itself is a town with its own Route 66 appeal, and the Sandhills Curiosity Shop is a testament to the hidden treasures that can be found in even the smallest of communities along the route.

Whether you're a Route 66 enthusiast, a lover of quirky attractions, or simply someone seeking an authentic and memorable experience, the Sandhills Curiosity Shop in Erick, Oklahoma, offers a delightful detour that captures the essence of the Mother Road's eccentric and welcoming spirit.

3. Meteor Crater, Winslow, Arizona:

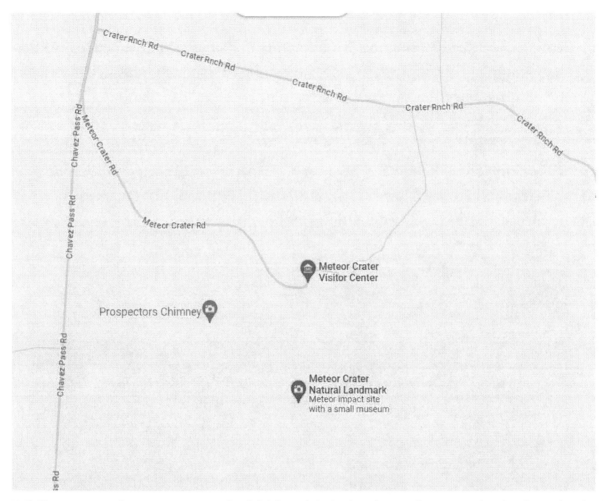

While Meteor Crater may not be hidden, it's indeed an often overlooked geological wonder along Route 66. Here's why you should make a point to visit this massive impact site and witness the evidence of a meteorite strike:

- Astronomical Impact: Meteor Crater is one of the best-preserved meteorite impact sites on Earth. It offers a unique opportunity to see the result of a cosmic collision that occurred around 50,000 years ago when a meteorite struck the Arizona desert.

- Massive Crater: The crater itself is awe-inspiring, measuring nearly one mile in diameter, over 2.4 miles in circumference, and about 550 feet deep. Its sheer size and the impact it created are difficult to comprehend until you stand on its rim.

- Educational Experience: Meteor Crater features an informative visitor center that offers insights into the science behind impact craters, meteorites, and the Earth's geological history. Interactive exhibits and educational displays make it an engaging stop for all ages.

- Scenic Views: From the rim of the crater, you can enjoy breathtaking panoramic views of the surrounding Arizona desert. It's a picturesque spot for taking photographs and appreciating the vastness of the American Southwest.

- Astronomy and Space Exploration: Meteor Crater has played a significant role in the study of impact craters and the moon's surface. It's also been used as a training ground for astronauts, making it a part of American space exploration history.

- Impressive Impact Features: While at Meteor Crater, you can see impact features such as the ejected rocks, known as "tektites," and the layers of rock that were disrupted by the meteorite's impact.

- Accessibility: Meteor Crater is conveniently located just off Interstate 40, making it a relatively easy and accessible detour from Route 66. It's an ideal place to stretch your legs, learn something new, and marvel at the forces of nature.

Meteor Crater is a testament to the Earth's dynamic history and the powerful forces at work in the universe. While it may not be hidden, its significance and scientific value make it a stop worth including in your Route 66 journey. It's a reminder that the road not only connects us to the past but also to the mysteries of the cosmos.

4. Blue Swallow Motel, Tucumcari, New Mexico:

Tucumcari is undeniably a Route 66 highlight, and the Blue Swallow Motel is a shining star in this classic town. Here's why the Blue Swallow Motel is not to be missed and why it's an excellent choice for a nostalgic overnight stay:

- Neon Nostalgia: The Blue Swallow Motel is a neon oasis on Route 66, with its iconic neon signs lighting up the night sky. Staying here is like stepping back in time to the heyday of the Mother Road when neon signs were the hallmark of roadside hospitality.

- Vintage Charm: The motel is a well-preserved relic of mid-20th-century Americana, with its cozy rooms and retro furnishings. It exudes the charm and character that make Route 66 motels so special.

- Personalized Service: The Blue Swallow is known for its friendly and accommodating owners who go out of their way to ensure guests have an enjoyable stay. They often provide Route 66 travel tips and recommendations to enhance your journey.

- Historical Significance: The motel has a rich history and has hosted countless travelers on their Route 66 adventures over the years. Its walls could tell stories of road trips, family vacations, and cross-country odysseys.

- Photographic Delight: The Blue Swallow Motel is a photographer's dream, both day and night. The neon signs, vintage cars, and well-preserved exterior make it a fantastic backdrop for capturing the essence of Route 66.

- Central Location: Tucumcari itself offers a variety of Route 66 attractions, including classic diners, historic landmarks, and murals that celebrate the road's history. The Blue Swallow's central location makes it a great base for exploring the town.

- Community Vibe: Staying at the Blue Swallow Motel provides a sense of connection with the Route 66 community. It's not just a place to rest; it's a place to share stories, swap travel tips, and connect with fellow road trippers.

- Night Sky Views: Tucumcari is known for its dark skies, making it an excellent spot for stargazing. Enjoy the quiet of the desert night and gaze at the stars while wrapped in the nostalgic ambiance of the Blue Swallow.

Whether you're seeking a memorable overnight stay, a dose of nostalgia, or a vibrant neon experience, the Blue Swallow Motel in Tucumcari, New Mexico, delivers on all fronts. It's a beacon of Route 66's past and a welcoming stop along the Mother Road.

5. Munger Moss Motel, Lebanon, Missouri:

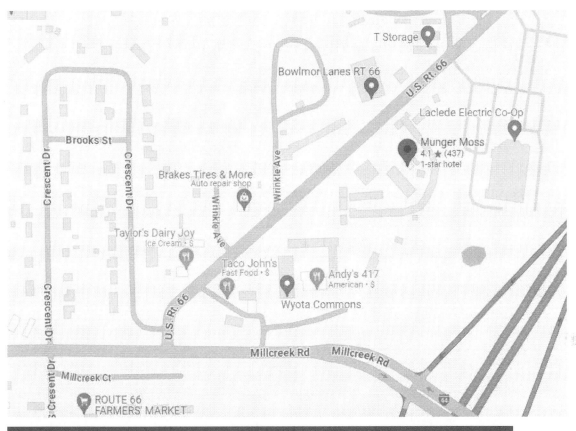

As you continue your journey along Route 66, the Munger Moss Motel in Lebanon, Missouri, is another vintage gem that promises a warm and nostalgic experience. Here's why this motel is worth considering for your Route 66 adventure:

- Classic Route 66 Atmosphere: The Munger Moss Motel embodies the classic Route 66 atmosphere that travelers seek on their journey. From the neon signage to the vintage furnishings, it's a step back in time to the golden era of the Mother Road.

- Friendly Owners: The motel is known for its friendly and welcoming owners who take pride in providing personalized service to guests. They often go the extra mile to ensure that travelers have a comfortable and enjoyable stay.

- Route 66 History: The Munger Moss Motel has a history deeply intertwined with Route 66. The owners are passionate about preserving the legacy of the road and are happy to share stories and insights about its history in Missouri.

- Comfortable Accommodations: While the motel retains its retro charm, it also offers comfortable and well-maintained accommodations. You can enjoy a cozy night's sleep in a room that harks back to the era of classic motels.

- Central Location: Lebanon is a convenient stop along Route 66, and the Munger Moss Motel's central location makes it an ideal base for exploring the town and its Route 66 attractions.

- Photo Opportunities: The motel's vintage aesthetics and neon signs provide excellent opportunities for capturing memorable photographs. It's a place where you can create lasting memories of your Route 66 journey.

- Route 66 Memorabilia: The Munger Moss Motel often features a collection of Route 66 memorabilia and artifacts that add to the overall experience. It's a place where the road's history comes alive.

- Community Feel: Staying at the Munger Moss Motel allows you to connect with other Route 66 travelers and share stories of the road. It's a part of the Route 66 community that embraces the camaraderie of the journey.

Whether you're a Route 66 enthusiast seeking authenticity, a fan of classic motels, or someone looking for a comfortable and friendly place to rest on your journey, the Munger Moss Motel in Lebanon, Missouri, offers a slice of the Mother Road's charm and history. It's a welcoming stop along the iconic highway, where the spirit of Route 66 lives on.

6. U-Drop Inn, Shamrock, Texas:

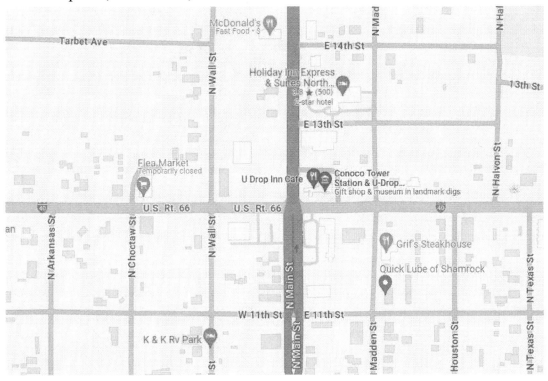

The U-Drop Inn in Shamrock, Texas, is a remarkable art deco gem that has been lovingly restored and transformed into more than just a roadside attraction—it's now a visitor center. Here's why this architectural highlight on Route 66 is a must-visit:

- Art Deco Masterpiece: The U-Drop Inn is a prime example of art deco architecture, characterized by its striking geometric shapes, bold colors, and intricate detailing. It's a visual delight that transports visitors to the glamor of the 1930s.

- Historical Significance: The U-Drop Inn has a rich history that dates back to the early days of Route 66. It served as a popular stop for weary travelers and truckers, offering fuel, food, and lodging. Its distinctive appearance made it an iconic landmark along the road.

- Restoration and Preservation: The restoration of the U-Drop Inn is a testament to the dedication of the local community and Route 66 enthusiasts. The building fell into disrepair but was lovingly restored to its former glory, ensuring that future generations can appreciate its architectural beauty.

- Visitor Center: Today, the U-Drop Inn houses a visitor center where you can learn about the history of Route 66 and its significance in American culture. The center provides valuable information for travelers and adds an educational dimension to your journey.

- Photo-Worthy: The U-Drop Inn is a photographer's dream. Its art deco façade and neon signs create stunning photo opportunities, both during the day and when illuminated at night. It's a place to capture the essence of Route 66 in images.

- Cultural Icon: The U-Drop Inn is more than just a building; it's a cultural icon that represents the spirit of adventure and exploration associated with Route 66. It's a place where the past meets the present on this historic highway.

- Local Hospitality: Shamrock is known for its friendly hospitality, and a visit to the U-Drop Inn is a chance to experience the warmth of the local community. The staff at the visitor center often provide helpful advice for Route 66 travelers.

- Café and Souvenirs: While at the U-Drop Inn, you can also enjoy a meal at the café and pick up Route 66 souvenirs to commemorate your journey.

The U-Drop Inn in Shamrock, Texas, is a testament to the enduring allure of Route 66 and the importance of preserving its historical landmarks. It's a place where you can appreciate the past, learn about the road's significance, and bask in the architectural beauty of a bygone era.

7. Santa Fe Loop, Albuquerque, New Mexico:

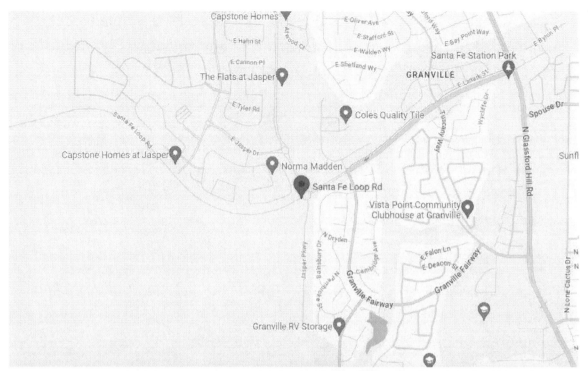

While many Route 66 travelers focus on the main route, there's a hidden gem known as the Santa Fe Loop that's worth exploring. Here's why you should consider taking this detour:

- Historical Significance: The Santa Fe Loop represents an earlier alignment of Route 66, showcasing the road's evolving history. Traveling this loop allows you to connect with the roots of the Mother Road and its importance in the development of the American Southwest.

- Scenic Beauty: This route offers picturesque landscapes and scenic vistas, making it a visual delight for nature enthusiasts and photographers. You'll pass through stunning desert terrain and experience the unique beauty of the Southwest.

- Native American Culture: The Santa Fe Loop provides opportunities to explore Native American culture and history. You can visit nearby reservations, pueblos, and cultural centers to learn about the rich traditions of indigenous peoples in the region.

- Artistic Hub: Albuquerque, often called the "Hot Air Balloon Capital of the World," is known for its vibrant arts scene. You can explore galleries, studios, and craft shops showcasing the work of local artists and artisans.

- Culinary Adventures: The Santa Fe Loop offers a chance to savor the flavors of New Mexican cuisine. Albuquerque and nearby Santa Fe are renowned for their delicious food, including dishes like green chile stew and sopapillas.

- Historic Sites: Along this route, you'll encounter historic sites that showcase the heritage of the Southwest. Whether it's Spanish colonial missions, old trading posts, or well-preserved adobe structures, there's no shortage of history to explore.

- Outdoor Activities: If you enjoy outdoor activities, the Santa Fe Loop provides access to hiking, biking, and even hot air ballooning. The region's mild climate and stunning landscapes make it an outdoor enthusiast's paradise.

- Hidden Treasures: While less traveled than the main route, the Santa Fe Loop holds its own hidden treasures, including unique roadside attractions, quirky museums, and unexpected surprises that add charm to your journey.

- Arts and Culture Festivals: Depending on the time of year, you might have the opportunity to participate in arts and culture festivals that celebrate the diversity and creativity of the region's residents.

Whether you're a history buff, a nature lover, an art aficionado, or someone who enjoys culinary delights, the Santa Fe Loop in Albuquerque, New Mexico, offers a multifaceted Route 66 experience. It's a detour that immerses you in the cultural richness and natural beauty of the American Southwest while connecting you with the heart of the Mother Road's legacy.

8. Cottonwood Canyon Road, Grand Staircase-Escalante National Monument, Utah:

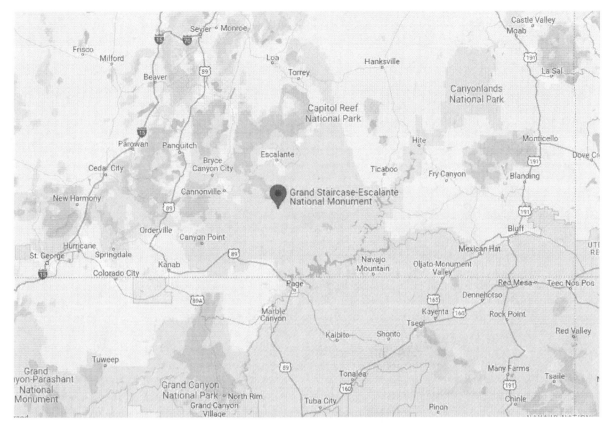

For the adventurous traveler seeking a taste of Utah's awe-inspiring natural beauty, a side trip along Cottonwood Canyon Road in the Grand Staircase-Escalante National Monument is a must. Here's why you should consider this detour:

- Unspoiled Wilderness: Cottonwood Canyon Road takes you deep into the heart of the Grand Staircase-Escalante National Monument, a vast wilderness known for its pristine landscapes, rugged canyons, and remote beauty. This is an opportunity to immerse yourself in the unspoiled splendor of the American West.

- Red Rock Canyons: The road winds through breathtaking red rock canyons, offering ever-changing vistas of towering cliffs, colorful sandstone formations, and the stunning geology that defines the region. It's a paradise for nature photographers and outdoor enthusiasts.

- Off the Beaten Path: Cottonwood Canyon Road is less traveled and less developed than many other parts of Route 66, providing a sense of solitude and adventure. It's an ideal escape for those seeking a break from the hustle and bustle of the more touristy sections of the road.

- Hiking and Exploration: There are numerous opportunities for hiking and exploration along the road. You can discover hidden slot canyons, scenic overlooks, and desert flora and fauna. Be sure to bring your hiking boots and a sense of adventure.

- Stargazing: The remote location of Cottonwood Canyon Road means minimal light pollution. It's an exceptional spot for stargazing, and the clear desert skies come alive with stars after dark.

- Photographic Opportunities: If you're a photographer, you'll find countless opportunities to capture the vivid landscapes, unique rock formations, and changing light conditions that make this area so captivating.

- Wildlife Encounters: Keep an eye out for the diverse wildlife that calls this region home. From desert bighorn sheep to coyotes, you might have a chance to observe some of Utah's native creatures in their natural habitat.

- Primitive Camping: Cottonwood Canyon Road offers primitive camping opportunities, allowing you to spend the night under the desert stars. Be sure to check regulations and come prepared with camping gear.

- Remote Serenity: This side trip offers a sense of remote serenity and a chance to disconnect from the modern world. It's an experience that can rejuvenate your spirit and provide a deep connection with nature.

- Caution: Since Cottonwood Canyon Road is an unpaved route, it's essential to check current road conditions, have a suitable vehicle (preferably high-clearance or 4x4), and carry ample supplies, including water and emergency provisions.

Venturing along Cottonwood Canyon Road in the Grand Staircase-Escalante National Monument is an opportunity to witness the raw beauty and rugged landscapes that define the American Southwest. It's a detour that promises adventure, solitude, and a deep appreciation for the natural wonders of Utah's red rock country.

These hidden gems add depth and character to your Route 66 adventure, allowing you to uncover the lesser-known stories and treasures along the Mother Road. Be sure to research their locations and hours of operation in advance to make the most of your visit.

Landmarks and Museums

Certainly, when exploring Route 66, there are numerous historic landmarks and museums that offer insights into the road's rich history and the communities it passes through. Here are some notable ones:

1. Route 66 State Park, Eureka, Missouri:

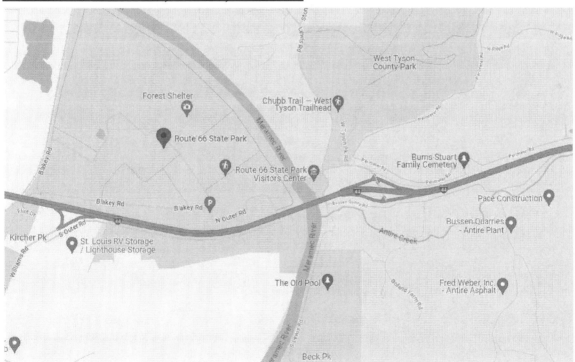

Located on the site of the former town of Times Beach, this park features a Route 66 museum and historic bridge. It offers hiking trails and a chance to learn about the road's history.

2. The Route 66 Association Hall of Fame and Museum, Pontiac, Illinois:

This museum celebrates the people, places, and events along Route 66. It showcases a wide range of memorabilia and artifacts.

3. National Route 66 Museum, Elk City, Oklahoma:

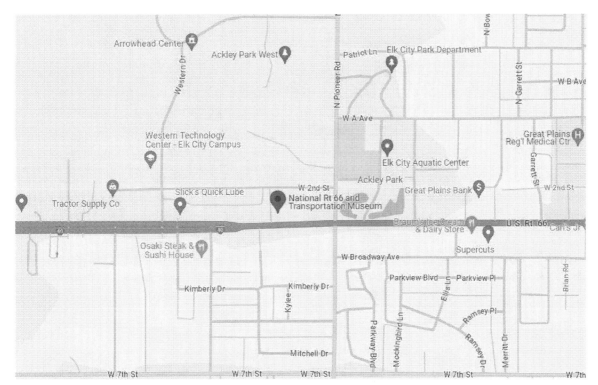

This museum is a comprehensive tribute to Route 66, featuring vintage vehicles, displays of roadside attractions, and a Hall of Fame recognizing notable figures in Route 66 history.

4. Barstow Route 66 Mother Road Museum, Barstow, California:

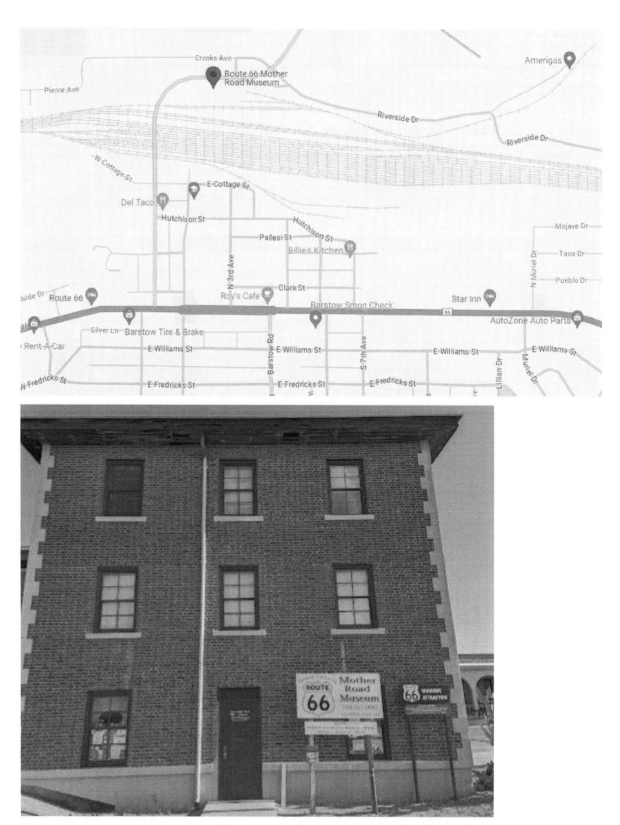

Located in a historic Harvey House, this museum explores the history of Route 66 through exhibits, artifacts, and photographs.

5. Route 66 Auto Museum, Santa Rosa, New Mexico:

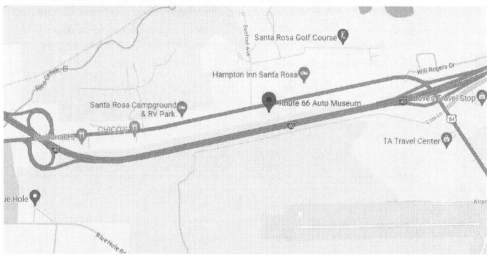

This museum features a diverse collection of vintage cars and Route 66 memorabilia, providing a nostalgic look at the road's heyday.

6. National Museum of American History, Washington, D.C.:

While not directly on Route 66, this Smithsonian museum houses the original "Main Street of America" sign from Chicago's Adams Street. It's a symbol of the road's cultural significance.

7. California Route 66 Museum, Victorville, California:

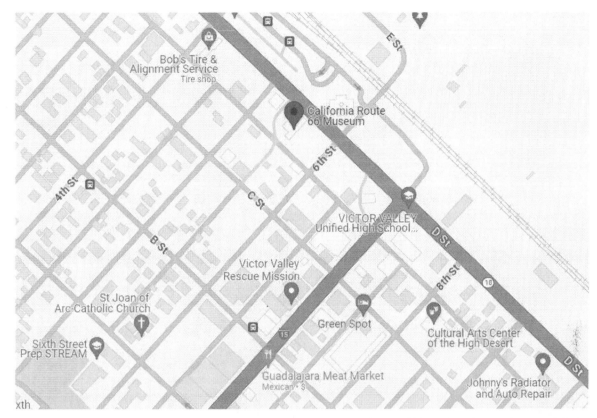

This museum focuses on the history of Route 66 in California, featuring exhibits on the road's evolution and the communities it passes through.

8. Museum of the American West, Los Angeles, California:

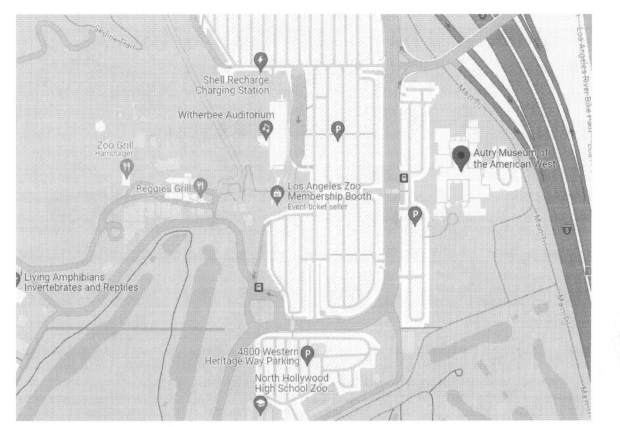

Located at the Autry Museum, this exhibit explores the impact of Route 66 on the American West, its role in migration, and its representation in popular culture.

9. Henry Ford Museum of American Innovation, Dearborn, Michigan:

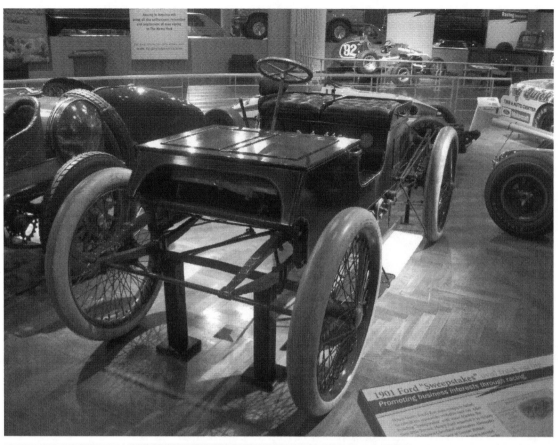

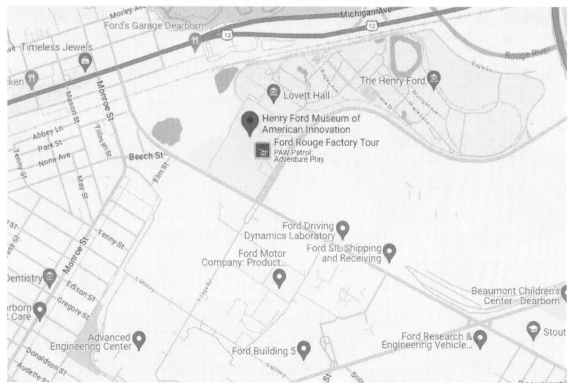

Although not solely dedicated to Route 66, this museum features items related to the road's history, such as vintage automobiles and roadside signs.

10. Route 66 Interpretive Center, Chandler, Oklahoma:

This center provides interactive exhibits that engage visitors in the story of Route 66 and its significance to American culture.

Visiting these historic landmarks and museums along Route 66 allows you to delve deeper into the road's history, its influence on American culture, and the communities that have thrived along its path. Each one offers a unique perspective on the Mother Road's enduring legacy.

Chapter 5: Accommodations and Dining

Route 66 Accommodation Overview

List of main states and cities with accommodation options for easy access (note that some are later explained in detail in the next subheading):

* Illinois:
 - Chicago (Starting Point)

Here's a list of accommodation options along Route 66 in Chicago:

- ☐ Chicago Motor Club Building (Hampton Inn Chicago Downtown/N Loop/Michigan Ave): This historic building in downtown Chicago has been converted into a Hampton Inn hotel. It's centrally located and offers comfortable accommodations with easy access to Route 66 attractions in the city.

- ☐ The Congress Plaza Hotel & Convention Center: Situated near Grant Park and Lake Michigan, The Congress Plaza Hotel is a historic landmark offering a range of rooms and suites. Its central location makes it convenient for exploring Route 66 landmarks in Chicago.

- ☐ The Palmer House, A Hilton Hotel: Located in the Loop district, The Palmer House is one of Chicago's oldest and most iconic hotels. It offers luxurious accommodations with historic charm, ideal for travelers exploring Route 66.

- ☐ Route 66 Hostel: For budget travelers, the Route 66 Hostel provides affordable dormitory-style accommodations in downtown Chicago. It's a great option for those looking to stay in a central location and meet other travelers.

 - Joliet

In Joliet, Illinois, along Route 66, there are several accommodation options conveniently located for travelers exploring the historic highway. Here are a few:

☐ Joliet Harrah's Casino & Hotel: This hotel is located near downtown Joliet, right off Interstate 80, making it easily accessible for travelers on Route 66. The casino hotel offers comfortable rooms, various dining options, and entertainment facilities like a casino and live entertainment.

☐ Best Western Joliet Inn & Suites: Situated off Interstate 55, this hotel is just a short drive from downtown Joliet and Route 66 attractions. It provides cozy rooms, complimentary breakfast, and amenities such as a fitness center and indoor pool.

☐ Hampton Inn by Hilton Joliet I-80: Conveniently located off Interstate 80, this Hampton Inn offers modern accommodations and easy access to Route 66 landmarks in Joliet. Guests can enjoy comfortable rooms, complimentary breakfast, and proximity to shopping and dining options.

☐ Red Roof Inn Joliet: This budget-friendly option is located off Interstate 55, offering affordable accommodations for travelers passing through Joliet on Route 66. The hotel provides basic amenities, including comfortable rooms and free Wi-Fi.

☐ Super 8 by Wyndham Joliet I-55 North: Another budget-friendly choice, this Super 8 motel is conveniently located off Interstate 55, making it a convenient stop for Route 66 travelers. The motel offers simple rooms, complimentary breakfast, and easy access to nearby attractions.

These accommodation options in Joliet provide travelers along Route 66 with convenient places to stay while exploring the historic highway and the attractions in the area.

-Springfield
In Springfield, Illinois, the capital city and a significant stop along Route 66, there are several accommodation options for travelers. Here are three examples:

- Route 66 Hotel & Conference Center: This hotel is located right on historic Route 66 and offers themed rooms that celebrate the nostalgia of the Mother Road. It's conveniently situated near many Route 66 attractions in Springfield, including the Illinois State Capitol and the Abraham Lincoln Presidential Library and Museum.

- State House Inn, Trademark Collection by Wyndham: Situated in downtown Springfield, this hotel provides comfortable accommodations with modern amenities. It's within walking distance of many Route 66 landmarks, such as the Old State Capitol and the Dana-Thomas House.

- Carpenter Street Hotel: Located near downtown Springfield, the Carpenter Street Hotel offers spacious rooms and suites, perfect for families or extended stays. It's close to Route 66 points of interest like the Cozy Dog Drive-In and the Shea's Gas Station Museum.

Missouri:
- St. Louis

In St. Louis, Missouri, another significant city along Route 66, there are several accommodation options for travelers. Here are three examples:

- The Cheshire: Located in the charming Clayton neighborhood of St. Louis, The Cheshire offers luxurious accommodations with a British-inspired theme. It's conveniently located near attractions like Forest Park, the St. Louis Zoo, and the Delmar Loop, making it a great base for exploring both Route 66 and the city's other landmarks.

- Moonrise Hotel: Situated in the vibrant Delmar Loop district, the Moonrise Hotel is a boutique hotel known for its modern design and unique amenities. Guests can enjoy rooftop views of the city, stylish rooms, and proximity to attractions such as the St. Louis Walk of Fame and the Pageant concert venue.

☐ The Westin St. Louis: This upscale hotel is located in downtown St. Louis, near the Gateway Arch and other iconic landmarks. It offers elegant rooms, a fitness center, and a rooftop pool with panoramic views of the city skyline. Its central location makes it convenient for travelers exploring Route 66 and the attractions in St. Louis.

- Rolla

In Rolla, Missouri, a city along Route 66, there are several accommodation options for travelers.

☐ Best Western Coachlight: Located right off Interstate 44, the Best Western Coachlight offers comfortable accommodations with easy access to Route 66. Guests can enjoy amenities such as a complimentary breakfast, outdoor pool, and free Wi-Fi. The hotel is conveniently situated near attractions like the Missouri University of Science and Technology and the Rolla Downtown Historic District.

☐ Baymont by Wyndham Rolla: This hotel provides affordable accommodations with a range of amenities including a fitness center, indoor pool, and complimentary breakfast. It's conveniently located off Interstate 44, making it a convenient stop for travelers exploring Route 66. The hotel is close to attractions like the Fugitive Beach recreational area and the Cedar Street Playhouse.

☐ Quality Inn Rolla: Situated off Interstate 44, the Quality Inn Rolla offers comfortable rooms and convenient amenities such as a fitness center, indoor pool, and complimentary breakfast. It's a great option for travelers passing through Rolla on Route 66, with easy access to attractions like the Memoryville USA Route 66 Car Museum and the Ozark Actors Theatre.

- Springfield

In Springfield, Missouri, another significant city along Route 66, there are several accommodation options for travelers. Here are three examples:

☐ Hotel Vandivort: Located in downtown Springfield, Hotel Vandivort offers boutique accommodations in a historic building. Guests can enjoy stylish rooms, a rooftop bar with panoramic views of the city, and amenities such as a fitness center and complimentary Wi-Fi. The hotel is conveniently situated near Route 66 attractions like the Birthplace of Route 66 Roadside Park and the Route 66 Car Museum.

☐ University Plaza Hotel & Convention Center: This hotel is located near Missouri State University and downtown Springfield, offering comfortable accommodations and amenities such as an outdoor pool, fitness center, and complimentary shuttle service to nearby attractions. It's a convenient base for travelers exploring Route 66 and the sights of Springfield, including the Wonders of Wildlife National Museum & Aquarium and the Springfield Art Museum.

☐ Best Western Route 66 Rail Haven: Situated along historic Route 66, this hotel offers retro-themed accommodations with a nod to the Mother Road's heyday. Guests can stay in vintage-style rooms adorned with Route 66 memorabilia and enjoy amenities like a seasonal outdoor pool and complimentary breakfast. The hotel is close to attractions like the Route 66 Springfield Visitor Center and the Fantastic Caverns.

These accommodation options in Springfield provide travelers with comfortable and convenient places to stay while experiencing Route 66 and the diverse attractions of the city.

* Kansas:
 - Galena
In Galena, Illinois, a charming town along Route 66, there are several accommodation options for travelers. Here are three examples:

☐ Goldmoor Inn: Located just outside Galena, the Goldmoor Inn offers luxurious accommodations in a scenic setting overlooking the Mississippi River. Guests can stay in elegantly appointed suites and cottages, dine at the onsite restaurant, and enjoy amenities such as in-room fireplaces and whirlpool tubs. The inn provides a tranquil retreat for travelers exploring Route 66 and the surrounding area.

☐ Chestnut Mountain Resort: Situated on a bluff overlooking the Mississippi River, Chestnut Mountain Resort offers comfortable accommodations with stunning views and easy access to outdoor activities such as skiing, hiking, and golfing. Guests can stay in lodge rooms or cozy villas and enjoy amenities like an indoor pool, hot tub, and onsite dining options. The resort is a great choice for travelers seeking adventure along Route 66.

☐ DeSoto House Hotel: Located in downtown Galena, the DeSoto House Hotel is one of the oldest operating hotels in Illinois, dating back to 1855. It offers charming accommodations with historic flair, including Victorian-style rooms and suites. Guests can explore the nearby shops, restaurants, and attractions of Galena's Main Street or relax in the hotel's cozy lobby and restaurant. The DeSoto House Hotel provides a memorable stay for travelers experiencing Route 66 and the historic charm of Galena.

* Oklahoma:

- Miami

Miami, Oklahoma, is a historic town along Route 66 with several accommodation options for travelers:

☐ Buffalo Run Casino & Resort: This resort-style casino hotel offers modern accommodations with amenities such as a casino floor, restaurants, entertainment venues, and a fitness center. Guests can enjoy spacious rooms and suites, as well as convenient access to gaming and dining options. The Buffalo Run Casino & Resort provides a lively atmosphere for travelers exploring Route 66 in Miami.

☐ Hampton Inn Miami: Located near Interstate 44, the Hampton Inn Miami offers comfortable accommodations with amenities such as a complimentary hot breakfast, indoor pool, and fitness center. It's a convenient choice for travelers passing through Miami on Route 66, with easy access to nearby attractions like the Dobson Museum and Route 66 Vintage Iron Motorcycle Museum.

☐ Holiday Inn Express & Suites Miami: Situated off Interstate 44, this Holiday Inn Express offers contemporary accommodations and convenient amenities such as a complimentary breakfast buffet, indoor pool, and fitness center. It's a great option for travelers seeking comfort and convenience while exploring Route 66 attractions in Miami and the surrounding area.

- Tulsa

In Tulsa, Oklahoma, a bustling city along Route 66, travelers can find a variety of accommodation options to suit their preferences. Here are three examples:

☐ The Mayo Hotel: This historic luxury hotel, located in downtown Tulsa, offers elegant accommodations and modern amenities. Guests can enjoy beautifully appointed rooms, fine dining options, a rooftop bar with stunning views of the city, and convenient access to Route 66 attractions such as the Blue Dome District and the Tulsa Arts District.

☐ Aloft Tulsa Downtown: Situated in the heart of downtown Tulsa, Aloft offers contemporary accommodations with a vibrant atmosphere. Guests can relax in stylish rooms featuring modern décor, enjoy amenities like an indoor pool and fitness center, and explore nearby attractions like the BOK Center and the Brady Arts District, both of which are within walking distance.

☐ Holiday Inn Express & Suites Tulsa Downtown: Conveniently located near downtown Tulsa and Route 66, this hotel offers comfortable rooms and suites along with complimentary breakfast, a fitness center, and an indoor pool. It provides easy access to attractions such as the Tulsa Zoo, Philbrook Museum of Art, and the historic Route 66 Meadow Gold Sign.

- Oklahoma City

In Oklahoma City, Oklahoma, travelers can find a variety of accommodation options conveniently located along Route 66 and near popular attractions:

☐ Ambassador Hotel Oklahoma City, Autograph Collection: Situated in the historic Midtown district, the Ambassador Hotel offers luxurious accommodations in a boutique setting. Guests can enjoy stylish rooms, a rooftop bar with panoramic views of downtown Oklahoma City, and amenities such as a fitness center and complimentary Wi-Fi. The hotel is close to Route 66 landmarks like the Milk Bottle Building and the Gold Dome.

☐ Renaissance Oklahoma City Convention Center Hotel: Located in the heart of downtown Oklahoma City, this hotel offers modern accommodations and easy access to Route 66 attractions such as the Oklahoma City National Memorial and Museum. Guests can enjoy spacious rooms, a fitness center, indoor pool, and onsite dining options.

☐ Hampton Inn & Suites Oklahoma City-Bricktown: Situated in the vibrant Bricktown entertainment district, this Hampton Inn offers comfortable accommodations and convenient access to Route 66 landmarks like the Oklahoma Route 66 Museum. Guests can explore nearby attractions such as the Chickasaw Bricktown Ballpark, Oklahoma City Museum of Art, and various dining and entertainment options within walking distance.

* Texas:
 - Amarillo

In Amarillo, Texas, a notable stop along Route 66, travelers can find a range of accommodation options to suit their needs:

☐ Big Texan Motel: Located adjacent to the iconic Big Texan Steak Ranch, this motel offers comfortable accommodations with a touch of western flair. Guests can stay in themed rooms decorated with rustic furnishings and enjoy amenities such as an outdoor pool and complimentary Wi-Fi. The motel is conveniently located off Interstate 40, making it easily accessible for travelers passing through Amarillo on Route 66.

☐ Drury Inn & Suites Amarillo: Situated near the Westgate Mall, this hotel offers modern accommodations and convenient amenities such as a complimentary hot breakfast, evening reception with free snacks and drinks, indoor pool, and fitness center. It's a great option for travelers seeking comfort and convenience while exploring Route 66 attractions in Amarillo.

☐ Courtyard by Marriott Amarillo Downtown: Located in downtown Amarillo, this hotel offers contemporary accommodations within walking distance of attractions like the Amarillo Civic Center Complex and the historic Route 66 Sixth Street Historic District. Guests can enjoy stylish rooms, a fitness center, onsite dining options, and easy access to nearby dining, shopping, and entertainment venues.

* New Mexico:
 - Tucumcari
In Tucumcari, New Mexico, a classic stop along Route 66, travelers can find a variety of accommodation options that capture the nostalgia and charm of the Mother Road. Here are three examples:

☐ Blue Swallow Motel: A beloved Route 66 landmark, the Blue Swallow Motel offers travelers a nostalgic experience with its vintage neon sign and retro accommodations. Guests can stay in restored rooms with classic furnishings and enjoy the motel's friendly hospitality. The Blue Swallow Motel is a must-visit for Route 66 enthusiasts seeking an authentic retro experience.

☐ La Cita Bed & Breakfast: This cozy bed and breakfast is located in a historic adobe building in downtown Tucumcari. Guests can enjoy comfortable rooms decorated with Southwestern flair, homemade breakfasts, and personalized hospitality from the innkeepers. La Cita Bed & Breakfast provides a tranquil retreat for travelers exploring Route 66 in Tucumcari.

☐ Historic Route 66 Motel: Situated on historic Route 66, this motel offers affordable accommodations with a retro vibe. Guests can stay in themed rooms decorated with vintage memorabilia and enjoy amenities such as free Wi-Fi and complimentary breakfast. The Historic Route 66 Motel provides a convenient and budget-friendly option for travelers passing through Tucumcari on the Mother Road.

These accommodation options in Tucumcari offer travelers a chance to experience the nostalgia and hospitality of Route 66 while exploring this iconic stretch of highway.

- Santa Rosa

In Santa Rosa, New Mexico, another significant stop along Route 66, travelers can find a variety of accommodation options offering comfort and convenience:

☐ Blue Hole RV Park: Located near the famous Blue Hole, a popular diving spot, this RV park offers spacious sites with full hookups and amenities such as showers, laundry facilities, and a picnic area. It's a great choice for travelers exploring Route 66 in Santa Rosa with their own accommodations.

☐ Route 66 Auto Museum & Gift Shop: This unique accommodation option allows guests to stay in themed rooms within the Route 66 Auto Museum. Each room is decorated with vintage cars and memorabilia, providing a nostalgic experience for guests. The museum also features a gift shop where visitors can purchase Route 66 souvenirs.

☐ Super 8 by Wyndham Santa Rosa: Situated near Interstate 40, this budget-friendly hotel offers comfortable rooms and convenient amenities such as complimentary breakfast, free Wi-Fi, and an outdoor pool. It's a convenient option for travelers passing through Santa Rosa on Route 66, with easy access to nearby attractions like the Blue Hole and the Route 66 Monument.

- Albuquerque

In Albuquerque, New Mexico, a vibrant city along Route 66, travelers can find a variety of accommodation options to suit their preferences. Here are three examples:

☐ Hotel Albuquerque at Old Town: Located near historic Old Town Albuquerque, this hotel offers luxurious accommodations with Southwestern flair. Guests can enjoy spacious rooms, onsite dining options, a swimming pool, and easy access to attractions like the Albuquerque Museum and the Indian Pueblo Cultural Center.

☐ Hotel Andaluz: This boutique hotel in downtown Albuquerque blends Spanish colonial architecture with modern amenities. Guests can stay in stylish rooms, dine at the onsite restaurant and rooftop bar, and relax in the hotel's luxurious ambiance. The hotel is conveniently located near Route 66 landmarks like the KiMo Theatre and the Route 66 Diner.

☐ El Vado Motel: Situated along Route 66 in Albuquerque's historic Route 66 neighborhood, El Vado Motel offers retro-style accommodations with a modern twist. Guests can stay in renovated rooms featuring mid-century furnishings and enjoy amenities such as a courtyard with food trucks, a swimming pool, and a beer garden. The motel is a great option for travelers seeking a nostalgic experience on the Mother Road.

- Gallup

In Gallup, New Mexico, a culturally rich city along Route 66, travelers can find a variety of accommodation options offering comfort and convenience;

☐ El Rancho Hotel & Motel: A historic landmark along Route 66, El Rancho Hotel & Motel offers travelers a unique lodging experience with its Old West charm and Hollywood history. Guests can stay in rooms named after famous guests like John Wayne and Ronald Reagan, dine at the onsite restaurant, and explore the hotel's collection of Western memorabilia.

☐ Best Western Plus Gallup Inn & Suites: Situated near Interstate 40, this hotel offers modern accommodations with amenities such as complimentary breakfast, an indoor pool, and a fitness center. It's a convenient choice for travelers passing through Gallup on Route 66, with easy access to attractions like the Gallup Cultural Center and the Rex Museum.

☐ Historic Route 66 Motel: Located along Route 66 in downtown Gallup, this motel offers affordable accommodations with a retro vibe. Guests can stay in themed rooms decorated with vintage memorabilia and enjoy amenities such as free Wi-Fi and complimentary breakfast. The Historic Route 66 Motel provides a convenient and budget-friendly option for travelers exploring the Mother Road in Gallup.

* Arizona:
 - Holbrook
In Holbrook, Arizona, a charming town along Route 66, travelers can find several accommodation options that capture the spirit of the Mother Road;

☐ Wigwam Motel: One of the most iconic lodging options along Route 66, the Wigwam Motel in Holbrook offers travelers a unique and nostalgic experience. Guests can stay in individual concrete teepee-shaped rooms, complete with vintage furnishings and modern amenities. The motel's retro ambiance and classic cars parked outside make it a must-visit for Route 66 enthusiasts.

☐ Best Western Arizonian Inn: Situated off Interstate 40, this hotel offers comfortable accommodations with amenities such as complimentary breakfast, an outdoor pool, and free Wi-Fi. It's a convenient choice for travelers passing through Holbrook on Route 66, with easy access to attractions like the Petrified Forest National Park and the Holbrook Historic District.

☐ Holbrook KOA Journey: For travelers seeking a more outdoor-oriented experience, the Holbrook KOA Journey offers RV sites, tent camping, and

134

cozy cabins. Guests can enjoy amenities such as a swimming pool, playground, and dog park, as well as organized activities like movie nights and pancake breakfasts. The campground provides a relaxing and scenic retreat along Route 66.

- Winslow

In Winslow, Arizona, a charming town immortalized in the famous Eagles song "Take It Easy," travelers can find several accommodation options offering comfort and convenience;

☐ La Posada Hotel: Located in a historic railroad hotel, La Posada offers travelers a unique and luxurious lodging experience. Guests can stay in beautifully restored rooms adorned with original artwork and Southwestern décor, dine at the onsite Turquoise Room restaurant, and explore the hotel's gardens and art galleries. La Posada Hotel is a must-visit for travelers seeking an unforgettable stay in Winslow.

☐ Best Western Plus Winslow Inn: Situated off Interstate 40, this hotel offers comfortable accommodations with amenities such as complimentary breakfast, an outdoor pool, and free Wi-Fi. It's a convenient choice for travelers passing through Winslow on Route 66, with easy access to attractions like Standin' on the Corner Park and the Old Trails Museum.

☐ Motel 10: A classic motor court motel located along Route 66, Motel 10 offers travelers retro-style accommodations with modern amenities. Guests can stay in rooms decorated with vintage furnishings and enjoy amenities such as free Wi-Fi and complimentary breakfast. The motel's convenient location and nostalgic ambiance make it a great choice for Route 66 enthusiasts.

- Flagstaff

In Flagstaff, Arizona, a vibrant city nestled in the Coconino National Forest and along the iconic Route 66, travelers can find a variety of accommodation options to suit their needs. Here are three examples:

☐ Hotel Monte Vista: Situated in downtown Flagstaff, Hotel Monte Vista is a historic landmark offering unique accommodations with a touch of vintage charm. Guests can stay in rooms adorned with retro furnishings and enjoy amenities such as an onsite bar, live music, and easy access to shops, restaurants, and attractions in the downtown area.

☐ Drury Inn & Suites Flagstaff: Located near Northern Arizona University and Interstate 40, this hotel offers modern accommodations and convenient amenities such as complimentary breakfast, an indoor pool, and a fitness center. It's a great option for travelers passing through Flagstaff on Route 66, with easy access to attractions like the Lowell Observatory and Walnut Canyon National Monument.

☐ Little America Hotel Flagstaff: Nestled amidst 500 acres of ponderosa pine forest, Little America Hotel Flagstaff offers travelers a tranquil retreat with upscale accommodations and amenities. Guests can stay in spacious rooms or suites, dine at the onsite restaurant, relax by the outdoor pool, and explore the hotel's scenic surroundings. The hotel is a convenient base for exploring Route 66 and nearby attractions like the Grand Canyon and Sedona.

- Williams

In Williams, Arizona, known as the "Gateway to the Grand Canyon" and a prominent stop along Route 66, travelers can find several accommodation options offering comfort and convenience:

☐ Grand Canyon Railway Hotel: Situated next to the historic Grand Canyon Railway Depot, this hotel offers cozy accommodations with a rustic ambiance. Guests can stay in rooms decorated in a Western theme, dine at the onsite restaurant, and enjoy amenities such as an indoor pool, hot tub, and fitness center. The hotel is a convenient base for travelers visiting the Grand Canyon and exploring Route 66 in Williams.

☐ Red Garter Inn: Located in a historic building in downtown Williams, the Red Garter Inn offers charming accommodations with a Victorian flair. Guests can stay in individually decorated rooms, enjoy a homemade breakfast, and explore the inn's quaint shops and galleries. The inn's central location makes it convenient for travelers exploring Route 66 landmarks and attractions in Williams.

☐ Canyon Motel & RV Park: This family-owned motel offers comfortable accommodations and RV sites in a scenic setting near downtown Williams. Guests can stay in cozy rooms decorated in a retro style, relax in the motel's courtyard, and enjoy amenities such as a hot tub and complimentary breakfast. The motel is a great option for travelers seeking a nostalgic experience along Route 66 in Williams.

- Kingman
In Kingman, Arizona, a historic town along Route 66, travelers can find several accommodation options offering comfort and convenience;

☐ El Trovatore Motel: A classic motor court motel located along Route 66, El Trovatore offers travelers a nostalgic experience with its retro-style accommodations and vintage charm. Guests can stay in themed rooms adorned with Route 66 memorabilia, enjoy amenities such as a swimming pool and barbecue area, and explore nearby attractions like the Route 66 Museum and the Mohave Museum of History & Arts.

☐ Best Western Plus A Wayfarer's Inn & Suites: Situated off Interstate 40, this hotel offers modern accommodations and convenient amenities such as complimentary breakfast, an outdoor pool, and free Wi-Fi. It's a great choice for travelers passing through Kingman on Route 66, with easy access to attractions like the Bonelli House and Historic Route 66.

☐ Hampton Inn & Suites Kingman: Located near Interstate 40 and Route 66, this hotel offers comfortable accommodations and amenities such as a complimentary hot breakfast, indoor pool, and fitness center. It's a convenient option for travelers exploring Kingman and nearby attractions like the Hualapai Mountain Park and the Kingman Railroad Museum.

* California:

- Needles

In Needles, California, a historic town located along Route 66 and the Colorado River, travelers can find several accommodation options offering comfort and convenience:

☐ Best Motel: Situated along historic Route 66, Best Motel offers travelers a convenient and budget-friendly lodging option in Needles. Guests can stay in comfortable rooms equipped with modern amenities such as free Wi-Fi and cable TV. The motel's central location makes it easy to explore Route 66 landmarks and nearby attractions like the Colorado River Museum.

☐ Rio Del Sol Inn Needles: Located near Interstate 40 and Route 66, Rio Del Sol Inn offers travelers comfortable accommodations and amenities such as a complimentary breakfast, outdoor pool, and hot tub. It's a convenient choice for travelers passing through Needles on Route 66, with easy access to attractions like the Needles Regional Museum and the historic El Garces Train Depot.

☐ Quality Inn Needles: Situated off Interstate 40, Quality Inn offers modern accommodations and convenient amenities such as complimentary breakfast, an outdoor pool, and free Wi-Fi. It's a great option for travelers exploring Route 66 in Needles, with easy access to attractions like the Route 66 Motel and the historic Bridge to Nowhere.

- Barstow

In Barstow, California, a historic town along Route 66 and a popular stop for travelers, there are several accommodation options offering comfort and convenience;

☐ Route 66 Motel: Located along historic Route 66, the Route 66 Motel offers travelers a nostalgic experience with its retro-style accommodations and vintage charm. Guests can stay in themed rooms adorned with Route 66 memorabilia, enjoy amenities such as free Wi-Fi and cable TV, and explore nearby attractions like the Route 66 Mother Road Museum and the Western America Railroad Museum.

☐ Comfort Suites Barstow near I-15: Situated near Interstate 15 and Route 66, Comfort Suites Barstow offers modern accommodations and convenient amenities such as a complimentary breakfast, indoor pool, and fitness center. It's a great choice for travelers passing through Barstow on Route 66, with easy access to attractions like the Barstow Station and the Mojave River Valley Museum.

☐ Quality Inn On Historic Route 66: Located along historic Route 66, Quality Inn offers comfortable accommodations and amenities such as complimentary breakfast, an outdoor pool, and free Wi-Fi. It's a convenient option for travelers exploring Route 66 in Barstow, with easy access to attractions like the Harvey House Railroad Depot and the Barstow Harvey House.

- Victorville

In Victorville, California, a city situated along historic Route 66, travelers can find several accommodation options offering comfort and convenience. Here are examples:

☐ Hawthorn Suites by Wyndham Victorville**: Located near Interstate 15 and Route 66, this hotel offers spacious suites with modern amenities such as fully equipped kitchens, complimentary breakfast, and free Wi-Fi. Guests can also enjoy the outdoor pool, fitness center, and barbecue area. The hotel provides a convenient base for travelers exploring Route 66 and nearby attractions.

☐ Motel 6 Victorville - Desert Express**: Situated off Interstate 15, this budget-friendly motel offers comfortable accommodations with amenities such as an outdoor pool and free morning coffee. It's a convenient option for travelers passing through Victorville on Route 66, with easy access to attractions like the California Route 66 Museum and the Route 66 Archway Monument.

☐ Comfort Suites Victorville: Located near Interstate 15 and Route 66, Comfort Suites offers modern accommodations and convenient amenities such as a complimentary breakfast, indoor pool, and fitness center. It's a great choice for travelers exploring Victorville and Route 66, with easy access to attractions like the Victor Valley Museum and the Mojave Narrows Regional Park.

These accommodation options in Victorville provide travelers with comfortable and convenient places to stay while experiencing Route 66 and the attractions of the area.

- San Bernardino
In San Bernardino, California, a city rich in history and culture along Route 66, travelers can find several accommodation options offering comfort and convenience. Here are examples:

☐ Route 66 Rendezvous Motel: Located along historic Route 66, Route 66 Rendezvous Motel offers travelers a nostalgic experience with its retro-style accommodations and vintage charm. Guests can stay in themed rooms adorned with Route 66 memorabilia, enjoy amenities such as free Wi-Fi and cable TV, and explore nearby attractions like the California Route 66 Museum and the historic McDonald's Museum.

☐ Hilton Garden Inn San Bernardino: Situated near Interstate 215 and Route 66, this hotel offers modern accommodations and convenient amenities such as a complimentary breakfast, outdoor pool, and fitness center. It's a great choice for travelers passing through San Bernardino on Route 66, with easy access to attractions like the Original McDonald's Site and the San Bernardino History and Railroad Museum.

☐ Hampton Inn & Suites San Bernardino: Located off Interstate 10 and Route 66, this hotel offers comfortable accommodations and amenities such as a complimentary breakfast, indoor pool, and free Wi-Fi. It's a convenient option for travelers exploring San Bernardino and Route 66, with easy access to attractions like the Inland Empire Military Museum and the historic Santa Fe Depot.

- Pasadena (Ending Point)

In Pasadena, California, a vibrant city known for its cultural attractions and historic landmarks, travelers can find several accommodation options offering comfort and convenience. Here are three examples:

☐ The Langham Huntington, Pasadena: Situated on 23 acres of lush gardens, this luxury hotel offers elegant accommodations and amenities such as a spa, outdoor pool, and several dining options. Guests can enjoy spacious rooms with luxurious furnishings, impeccable service, and easy access to attractions like the Huntington Library, Art Museum, and Botanical Gardens.

☐ Sheraton Pasadena Hotel: Located in downtown Pasadena, this modern hotel offers comfortable accommodations and convenient amenities such as a fitness center, outdoor pool, and onsite dining options. It's a great choice for travelers exploring Pasadena's vibrant culture and attractions like the Pasadena Museum of California Art and the Norton Simon Museum.

☐ Residence Inn by Marriott Los Angeles Pasadena/Old Town: Situated near Old Town Pasadena, this extended-stay hotel offers spacious suites with fully equipped kitchens and separate living areas. Guests can enjoy amenities such as complimentary breakfast, a fitness center, and outdoor patio with fire pits. The hotel provides a convenient base for exploring Pasadena's historic sites, shopping districts, and dining options.

Accommodation Options Along Route 66

Along the iconic Route 66, you'll find a diverse range of accommodation options to suit various preferences and budgets. Here's an overview of the types of accommodations you can expect to encounter on your journey:

1.Classic Motels: One of the most iconic aspects of a Route 66 journey is the opportunity to stay in classic motels that hearken back to the road's heyday in the mid-20th century. These motels are like time capsules, offering travelers a chance to experience the nostalgia and charm of a bygone era. They often feature retro decor, including vintage furnishings, neon signs that light up the night, and distinctive architectural styles that reflect the spirit of the road. Staying in these motels is like taking a step back in time, where you can immerse yourself in the history and culture of Route 66. It's an authentic and memorable way to connect with the road's enduring legacy and the travelers who came before you.

- Modern Comforts: While classic motels evoke a sense of nostalgia, it's important to note that many of them have been lovingly restored and updated to provide modern comforts. Travelers can expect clean and well-maintained rooms, comfortable beds, and amenities like Wi-Fi and cable TV. This blend of vintage charm and contemporary convenience ensures that your stay is not only nostalgic but also comfortable.

- Neon Nights: Neon signage is a hallmark of classic Route 66 motels. These neon signs come to life as the sun sets, casting a warm and inviting glow that beckons travelers to stop and rest. The sight of neon lights illuminating the roadside is a quintessential Route 66 experience, and it's a reminder of the road's role as the "Main Street of America" in its heyday.

- Roadside Culture: Classic motels are an integral part of Route 66's roadside culture. They often feature whimsical and eye-catching architectural elements, such as wigwam-shaped rooms or themed decor that reflects the local surroundings. These motels were designed to capture the imagination of travelers and provide a sense of adventure and novelty along the journey.

- <u>Preserving History:</u> Many Route 66 enthusiasts and preservationists are dedicated to maintaining and restoring these classic motels. Staying in them not only allows you to enjoy a unique travel experience but also supports the ongoing efforts to preserve the heritage of the Mother Road. It's a way to contribute to the continued existence of these iconic landmarks for future generations to enjoy.

In summary, classic motels along Route 66 offer travelers a chance to step back in time, experience the nostalgia of the road's golden era, and immerse themselves in its rich history and culture. They blend vintage charm with modern comforts, making them a memorable and authentic part of any Route 66 adventure. While there are numerous classic motels along the route, here are a few notable examples:

<u>1. Blue Swallow Motel (Tucumcari, New Mexico):</u>

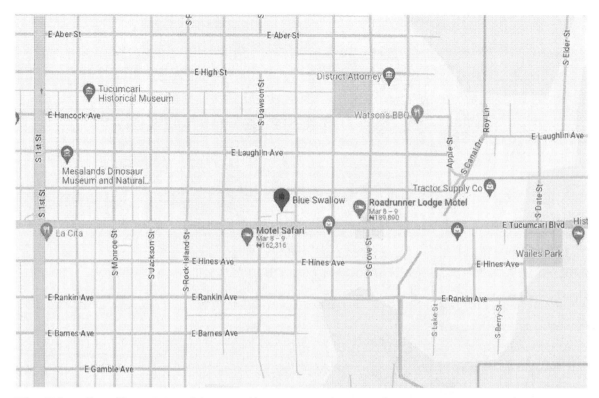

The Blue Swallow Motel is a well-preserved gem along Route 66. It features a classic neon sign, vintage furnishings, and a friendly atmosphere. This motel has been a favorite among Route 66 travelers for generations.

2. Wigwam Motel (Holbrook, Arizona):

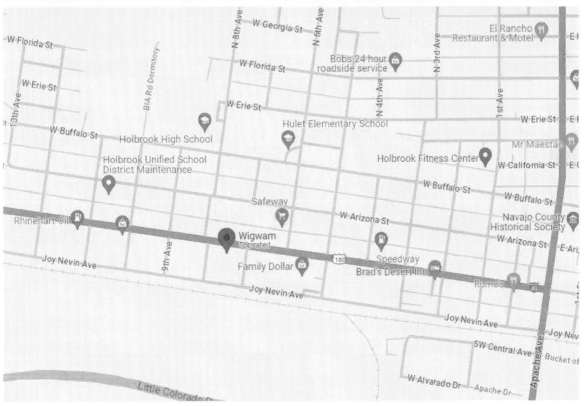

The Wigwam Motel is iconic for its unique wigwam-shaped rooms. Guests can stay in these cozy and kitschy accommodations while enjoying a taste of Route 66 history.

Remember that many classic motels along Route 66 have limited availability, so it's a good idea to book in advance if you plan to stay at one of these iconic spots. Staying in a classic motel is not just about accommodation but also about immersing yourself in the history and culture of the Mother Road.

2. Modern Hotels: While classic motels hold a special place along Route 66, travelers who seek modern comforts and amenities will find a diverse array of hotels available along the route. Here's what you can expect from modern hotels on your Route 66 journey:

- Contemporary Comfort: Modern hotels are designed with the comfort and convenience of today's travelers in mind. They offer well-appointed rooms with comfortable beds, modern furnishings, and updated amenities. Air conditioning, flat-screen TVs, and Wi-Fi access are commonly provided to ensure a comfortable and connected stay.

- Chain Hotels: Along major stops and cities on Route 66, you'll often encounter well-known chain hotels. These hotels, part of nationwide or global networks, offer consistency in quality and service. Travelers who are members of loyalty programs may find these options appealing for the familiarity and perks they provide.

- Boutique Accommodations: In addition to chain hotels, Route 66 also boasts boutique accommodations. These smaller, independently owned hotels often feature unique and stylish decor, reflecting the character of the local area. Staying in a boutique hotel can add a touch of charm and personality to your journey.

- Amenities: Modern hotels frequently provide a range of amenities to enhance your stay. Depending on the property, you may have access to fitness centers, swimming pools, on-site restaurants, and room service. These amenities can make your stay more enjoyable and convenient.

- Location: Modern hotels are typically situated in convenient locations along Route 66, making it easy to access key attractions, restaurants, and services. Whether you're exploring a vibrant city or a scenic stretch of the road, you'll often find modern hotel options nearby.

- Consistency: For travelers who value predictability and a uniform level of service, modern hotels deliver a consistent experience. This can be reassuring when you're on a long road trip and want a reliable place to rest each night.

- Booking Flexibility: Modern hotels often offer flexible booking options, allowing travelers to make reservations online or by phone. This flexibility can be especially valuable when planning a Route 66 journey, as it allows you to secure your accommodations in advance.

While classic motels evoke the nostalgia of a bygone era, modern hotels cater to the needs and preferences of contemporary travelers. They provide a comfortable and reliable lodging option, ensuring that you have a comfortable place to stay as you explore the diverse landscapes and communities along Route 66. Whether you choose a well-known chain hotel or a charming boutique property, modern hotels are an integral part of the Route 66 experience.

Here are some examples of modern hotels along Route 66:

1. Hyatt Regency St. Louis at The Arch (St. Louis, Missouri):

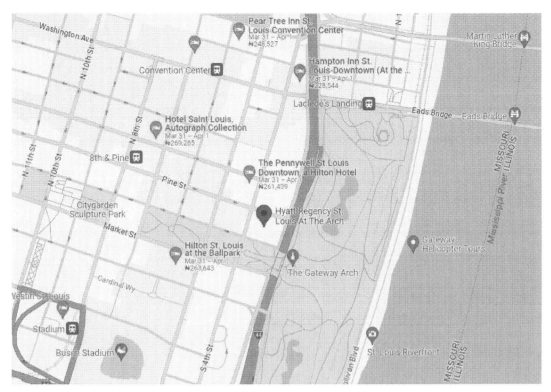

Located near the Gateway Arch, this modern hotel offers upscale rooms and stunning views of the Arch and the Mississippi River.

2. The Wigwam (Litchfield Park, Arizona):

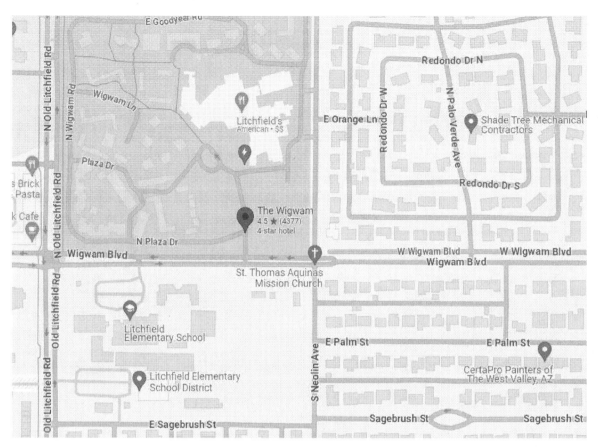

Although associated with the classic Wigwam Motel, The Wigwam in Litchfield Park offers modern resort-style accommodations, including golf, a spa, and luxury rooms.

3. Embassy Suites by Hilton Amarillo Downtown (Amarillo, Texas):

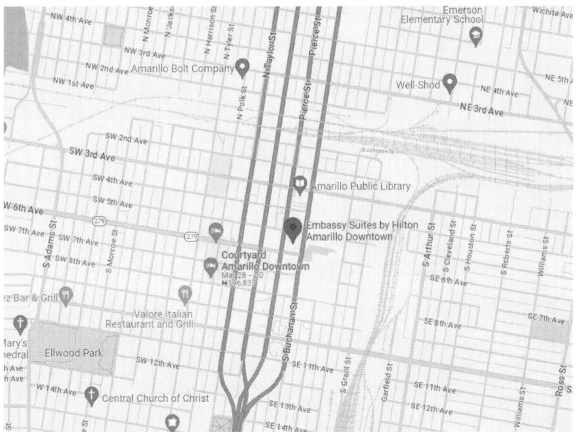

This contemporary hotel in downtown Amarillo offers spacious suites, an indoor pool, and a complimentary evening reception.

4. Hotel Andaluz Albuquerque (Albuquerque, New Mexico):

A boutique hotel in downtown Albuquerque, Hotel Andaluz combines modern luxury with historic charm. It's known for its stylish rooms and rooftop bar.

5. Hotel Chicago Downtown, Autograph Collection (Chicago, Illinois):

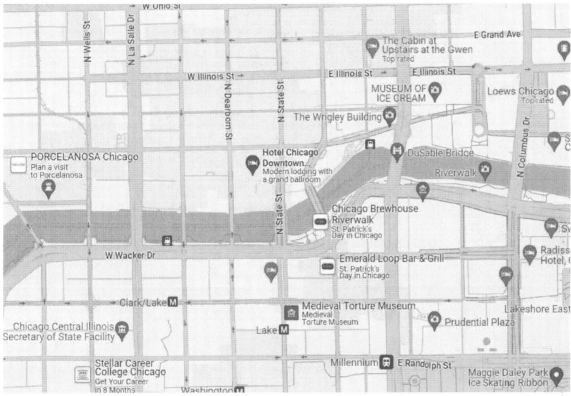

Located in the heart of downtown Chicago, this modern hotel is within walking distance of attractions like Millennium Park and the Art Institute of Chicago.

3. Bed and Breakfasts: Along Route 66, travelers have the delightful option of staying in charming bed and breakfasts. These establishments offer a distinct and intimate lodging experience that's characterized by the following features:

- Quaint Atmosphere: Bed and breakfasts are often located in historic homes, cottages, or inns, which exude a cozy and inviting ambiance. The decor is carefully curated to create a homey and comfortable setting that's perfect for relaxation.

- Personalized Service: One of the defining traits of bed and breakfasts is the personalized service provided by innkeepers. These hosts are typically attentive and eager to make your stay memorable. They can offer local insights, recommendations for nearby attractions, and cater to specific guest preferences.

- Unique Rooms: Each room in a bed and breakfast is usually uniquely decorated, offering a variety of themes and styles. This variety allows travelers to choose accommodations that suit their tastes, whether they prefer a romantic, vintage, or contemporary setting.

- Homemade Breakfast: As the name suggests, breakfast is a highlight of the bed and breakfast experience. Guests can look forward to a delicious, homemade morning meal that often includes freshly baked goods, locally sourced ingredients, and creative culinary offerings. It's a delightful way to start the day.

- Local Hospitality: Staying in a bed and breakfast provides an opportunity to connect with the local community and experience genuine hospitality. Innkeepers often have deep roots in the area and can share stories, traditions, and insights about Route 66 and the surrounding region.

- Intimate Setting: Bed and breakfasts are typically smaller and more intimate compared to larger hotels. This creates a sense of tranquility and privacy, making them ideal for couples seeking a romantic getaway or anyone desiring a peaceful retreat.

- Historic and Quirky Properties: Along Route 66, you may come across bed and breakfasts housed in historic buildings, such as old railway depots or charming Victorian homes. Some establishments also embrace Route 66's quirky side by offering unique and themed accommodations.

- Local Recommendations: Innkeepers are excellent resources for discovering local attractions, dining options, and hidden gems. They can help you plan your Route 66 adventure by providing insider tips and advice.

- Booking Directly: Many bed and breakfasts encourage travelers to book directly through their websites or by phone. This direct booking method allows guests to communicate directly with the innkeepers, ensuring a personalized experience.

Bed and breakfasts along Route 66 offer a blend of comfort, character, and genuine hospitality. Whether you're seeking a romantic getaway, a quiet escape, or a chance to connect with local culture, these charming accommodations provide a memorable and authentic stay along the Mother Road.

Here are a few examples of B&Bs along Route 66:

1. Starlight Pines Bed & Breakfast (Flagstaff, Arizona):

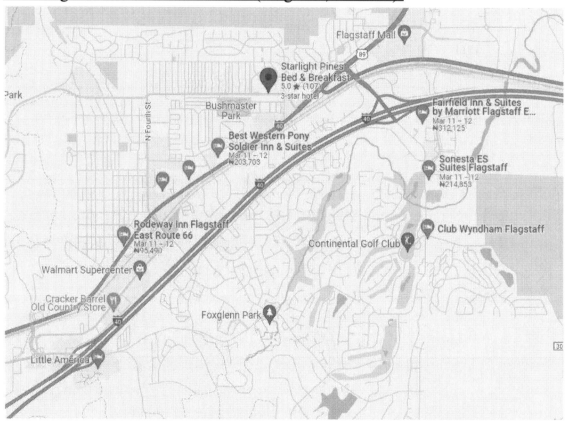

Nestled in Flagstaff, Arizona, this B&B provides a peaceful retreat in a forested area. Guests can enjoy comfortable rooms, delicious breakfasts, and easy access to Route 66 and the Grand Canyon.

3. Rouge's Manor (Eureka Springs, Arkansas):

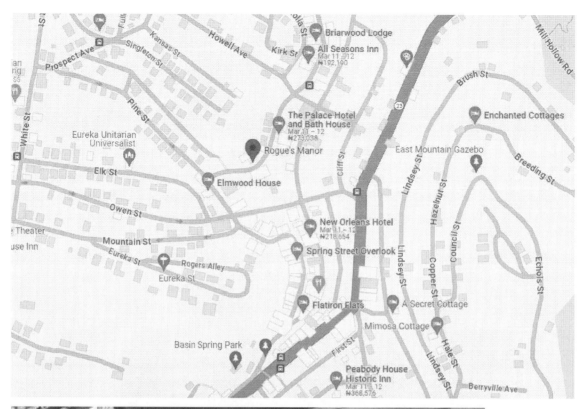

Eureka Springs, Arkansas, is not directly on Route 66, but it's a popular stop for travelers. Rouge's Manor is a Victorian-style B&B with elegant rooms and a romantic atmosphere.

4. Old Caledonian Bed & Breakfast (Caledonia, Missouri):

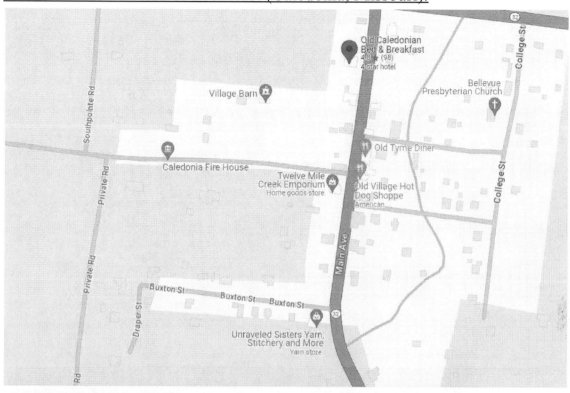

Located in the charming town of Caledonia, Missouri, this B&B offers comfortable accommodations in a historic building. It's a peaceful place to unwind after a day of exploring Route 66.

5. Pueblo Bonito Bed & Breakfast Inn (Santa Fe, New Mexico):

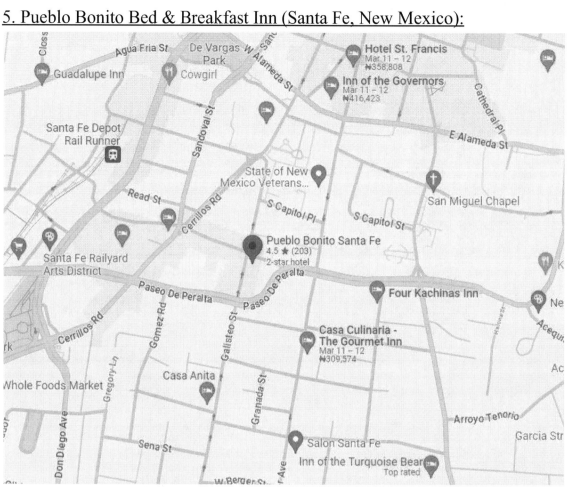

Santa Fe is a bit off the Route 66 path, but it's a city worth visiting. The Pueblo Bonito B&B Inn combines Southwestern charm with comfortable rooms and is an excellent base for exploring Santa Fe.

4. Vacation Rentals: For travelers seeking independence, space, and a home-away-from-home experience along Route 66, vacation rentals are an excellent option. Here's what you can expect from vacation rentals on your Route 66 journey:

- Diverse Accommodations: Vacation rentals encompass a wide range of options, including cottages, cabins, apartments, condos, and even entire homes. This diversity allows travelers to choose accommodations that suit their group size, preferences, and budget.

- Privacy and Independence: One of the primary advantages of vacation rentals is the level of privacy and independence they offer. Guests can enjoy the entire rental property to themselves, creating a sense of home and allowing for flexibility in daily routines.

- Fully Equipped Kitchens: Many vacation rentals feature fully equipped kitchens, complete with appliances and cookware. This amenity is particularly appealing to travelers who enjoy preparing their meals, whether it's a quick breakfast before hitting the road or a family dinner.

- Living Spaces: Vacation rentals typically include separate living spaces, such as a living room or common area. These spaces provide comfort and relaxation after a day of exploring Route 66's attractions.

- Local Immersion: Staying in a vacation rental often provides a more immersive experience in the local community. You'll have the opportunity to shop at local markets, interact with neighbors, and get a taste of everyday life along the route.

- Cost-Effective for Groups: Vacation rentals can be cost-effective, especially for groups or families traveling together. Splitting the cost of a rental property can often be more budget-friendly than booking multiple hotel rooms.

- Flexibility: Vacation rentals offer flexibility in terms of check-in and check-out times, making them suitable for travelers with varying schedules. Additionally, they can be booked for shorter or longer stays, accommodating both weekend getaways and extended road trips.

- Pets Welcome: Many vacation rentals are pet-friendly, allowing you to bring along your furry companions on your Route 66 adventure.

- Scenic Locations: Route 66 passes through picturesque landscapes, and vacation rentals can be found in scenic locations. Whether you prefer a cabin in the woods, a beachfront condo, or a downtown apartment, you can choose a rental property that aligns with your ideal setting.

- Booking Platforms: Vacation rentals can be easily booked through online platforms and websites. Popular vacation rental platforms offer a wide selection of properties, complete with photos, descriptions, and guest reviews to help you make informed decisions.

Here are a few examples of vacation rentals you might encounter along the route:

1. Airbnb:
Airbnb offers a wide range of vacation rental options, from cozy cabins to historic homes. You can find Airbnb properties in many towns and cities along Route 66, allowing you to immerse yourself in the local culture.

2. Vrbo (Vacation Rentals by Owner): Vrbo features vacation homes, cottages, and
condos available for rent along the route. These properties often provide more space and privacy than traditional hotels.

3. HomeAway: HomeAway, which is now part of Vrbo, offers vacation rentals in
various sizes and styles. You can find unique properties like desert retreats or charming bungalows to enhance your Route 66 experience.

4. Vacasa: Vacasa manages vacation rental properties in several Route 66
destinations. Their professional property management ensures a smooth stay, and you can choose from a variety of homes that suit your preferences.

5. FlipKey: FlipKey, a TripAdvisor company, provides access to vacation rentals
and private homes along Route 66. You can read reviews from previous guests to help you make informed decisions.

When booking vacation rentals along Route 66, be sure to check the property's amenities, location, and reviews to ensure it meets your needs and expectations. Whether you're seeking a rustic cabin in the woods or a spacious home in a vibrant city, you'll likely find a vacation rental that suits your preferences along this iconic highway.

Other Accommodation Options
5. Themed and Unique Lodging: As you journey along Route 66, you'll encounter a captivating array of themed and unique lodging options that add an extra layer of adventure and personality to your trip. These accommodations are a

testament to the road's enduring spirit of creativity and individuality. Here's what you can expect from themed and unique lodging experiences:

- Novelty Accommodations: Route 66 is home to some of the quirkiest and most imaginative lodging options you'll find anywhere. These accommodations take creativity to new heights, featuring themed rooms or structures that transport you to a different world. Examples include wigwam-shaped motel rooms, teepees, train cabooses, and even underground cave lodgings.

- A Taste of History: Many themed lodgings pay homage to Route 66's rich history and culture. You might stay in a vintage motor court motel that has been lovingly restored to its mid-20th-century glory. These properties provide a tangible connection to the road's past and offer a unique glimpse into the heyday of Route 66 travel.

- Local Flavor: Route 66's charm lies in its diversity, and themed accommodations often reflect the local culture and heritage of the area in which they are located. You can find lodgings that incorporate Native American, Western, or retro Americana themes, adding an element of cultural immersion to your journey.

- Vintage Airstreams: Airstream trailers have become synonymous with the American road trip, and some Route 66 towns offer the opportunity to stay in beautifully restored vintage Airstreams. These silver bullets provide a blend of nostalgia and comfort, making them a unique and Instagram-worthy choice for travelers.

- Artistic Expressions: Route 66 is a canvas for artistic expression, and some accommodations embrace this ethos. You might encounter lodgings adorned with vibrant murals, sculptures, or other forms of public art that reflect the creative spirit of the road.

- Authenticity and Atmosphere: Themed and unique lodgings are designed to immerse you in a specific atmosphere or time period. Whether it's the Old

West, the Route 66 of the 1950s, or a kitschy retro diner, these accommodations provide an immersive experience that complements your road trip adventure.

- Photo Opportunities: Staying in themed lodgings often means you'll have the opportunity to take memorable photos that capture the essence of Route 66. The novelty and character of these accommodations make for excellent photo backdrops and lasting memories.

- Booking in Advance: Due to their popularity and limited availability, it's advisable to book themed and unique lodging well in advance, especially during peak travel seasons. This ensures you secure the accommodation that aligns with your Route 66 vision.

Themed and unique lodging options along Route 66 add an element of fun, surprise, and authenticity to your journey. Whether you're seeking a cozy stay in a historic wigwam or an adventure in a themed trailer park, these accommodations turn your road trip into an unforgettable experience.

6. Campgrounds and RV Parks: For travelers who appreciate the beauty of the great outdoors and seek a more rustic experience along Route 66, campgrounds and RV parks provide an excellent choice. Here's what you can expect from these natural accommodations on your Route 66 adventure:

- Close-to-Nature Experience: Campgrounds and RV parks allow you to immerse yourself in the natural landscapes along Route 66. You can pitch a tent beneath the stars, park your RV amidst scenic vistas, or even rent a cabin in some locations. These options provide an intimate connection with the environment.

- Variety of Settings: Route 66 passes through a wide range of landscapes, and campgrounds and RV parks are strategically located to offer diverse settings. You can camp in lush forests, alongside serene lakes, in the heart of the desert, or near historic landmarks, each providing a unique atmosphere for your stay.

- Basic Amenities: Campgrounds typically offer basic amenities, such as restrooms, showers, and picnic areas. RV parks often provide full hook-up services, including water, electricity, and sewage disposal, making them suitable for self-contained travel.

- Affordability: Camping is often a cost-effective lodging option, especially for travelers on a budget. Campground and RV park fees are typically lower than hotel or motel rates, allowing you to allocate more of your budget to other aspects of your Route 66 journey.

- Outdoor Activities: Being in the midst of nature opens up opportunities for outdoor activities. You can hike scenic trails, fish in nearby lakes or rivers, have a barbecue, and simply enjoy the tranquility of the outdoors. Many campgrounds also offer recreational facilities.

- Social Atmosphere: Campgrounds and RV parks can foster a sense of community among travelers. You may have the chance to meet fellow road trippers, share stories around the campfire, and exchange travel tips.

- Stargazing: Route 66 often traverses remote areas with minimal light pollution, making campgrounds and RV parks ideal spots for stargazing. On clear nights, you can marvel at the brilliance of the night sky and constellations.

- Pet-Friendly: Many campgrounds and RV parks are pet-friendly, allowing you to bring your furry companions along on your adventure.

- Reservations: While some campgrounds and RV parks offer first-come, first-served sites, it's advisable to make reservations in advance, especially during peak travel seasons. This ensures you have a designated spot waiting for you at your chosen location.

Along Route 66, there are numerous campgrounds and RV parks that cater to travelers seeking a more outdoorsy experience. Here is an example:

Canyon Gateway RV Park -

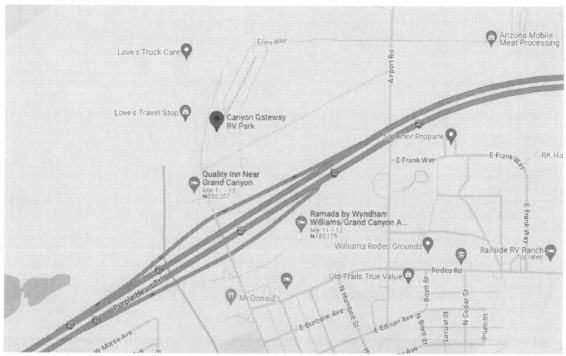

Located in Williams, Arizona, this RV park offers a picturesque setting near the entrance to the Grand Canyon. It provides spacious RV sites with full hookups, as well as amenities such as laundry facilities, showers, and a convenience store.

Guests can enjoy easy access to hiking trails, scenic drives, and other attractions in the area.

Whether you're an avid camper, an RV enthusiast, or simply looking to connect with nature along Route 66, campgrounds and RV parks offer a serene and budget-friendly lodging option. They provide a refreshing break from the road's hustle and bustle and allow you to fully appreciate the natural beauty that surrounds this historic route.

7. Historic Inns:

Route 66 is a treasure trove of history, and some towns along the route are home to historic inns and lodges that have been welcoming travelers for generations. These establishments offer a unique and nostalgic lodging experience, characterized by the following features:

- Timeless Charm: Historic inns and lodges often occupy buildings with rich architectural character and historical significance. The decor and ambiance reflect a bygone era, providing a charming and atmospheric stay.

- Antique Furnishings: The interiors of these accommodations are typically adorned with antique furnishings, period-appropriate decor, and memorabilia that transport guests back in time. Staying in such settings can feel like stepping into a living museum.

- Local Stories: Innkeepers and staff at historic lodgings often have deep connections to the community and a wealth of knowledge about Route 66's history. They can share fascinating stories, recommend local attractions, and enhance your understanding of the road's heritage.

- Unique Rooms: Each room in a historic inn is often uniquely decorated, offering a sense of individuality and character. Guests can choose accommodations that resonate with their preferences, whether it's a room with vintage charm or a suite with a touch of luxury.

- Historical Significance: Some historic inns have played a role in Route 66's past, serving as rest stops, meeting points, or landmarks along the way. Staying in these lodgings provides a direct connection to the road's history.

- Personalized Service: Historic inns prioritize personalized service and attention to detail. Innkeepers are often passionate about preserving the property's heritage and ensuring that guests have a memorable and comfortable stay.

- Local Cuisine: Many historic inns feature on-site restaurants that serve regional and traditional cuisine. Dining at these establishments can be a culinary journey that complements your overall Route 66 experience.

- Cozy Atmosphere: The smaller size of historic inns and lodges fosters a cozy and intimate atmosphere. Guests can unwind in communal spaces, chat with fellow travelers, or simply relax by the fireplace.

- Scenic Locations: These accommodations are often situated in picturesque locations along Route 66, offering scenic views and proximity to key attractions. Whether it's a hillside inn with panoramic vistas or a lodge nestled in the heart of a charming town, the settings are often memorable.

- Booking in Advance: Due to their popularity and limited availability, it's advisable to book historic inns in advance, especially if you have your heart set on a particular property. This ensures you secure a room in these cherished and sought-after lodgings.

El Rancho Hotel -
Situated in Gallup, New Mexico, the El Rancho Hotel is a historic inn that has hosted countless celebrities and dignitaries since its opening in 1937. Designed in the style of a grand Southwestern hacienda, the hotel features a beautiful courtyard and lobby adorned with Native American art and artifacts. Guests can stay in rooms named after famous guests such as John Wayne and Ronald Reagan, and enjoy amenities like an indoor swimming pool and onsite restaurant.

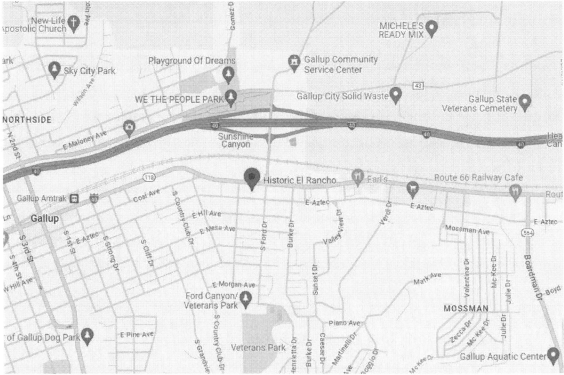

Staying in a historic inn along Route 66 allows you to experience the road's past in a tangible and immersive way. These lodgings are a testament to the enduring allure of the Mother Road, where history, nostalgia, and warm hospitality converge to create an unforgettable journey.

8. **Route 66 Associations:** Along Route 66, you'll find a network of dedicated Route 66 associations and preservation groups that are deeply committed to safeguarding the road's history and culture. These organizations often operate lodging properties that not only offer travelers a unique place to stay but also contribute directly to the preservation of Route 66's heritage. Here's what you can expect when staying at properties affiliated with these associations:

- Passion for Preservation: Properties operated by Route 66 associations are typically infused with a passion for preserving the road's history. The owners and staff often have a profound knowledge of Route 66's significance and are dedicated to maintaining the authenticity and character of their lodgings.

- Historic Significance: Many of these properties have historical significance related to Route 66, whether they were former motor courts, roadside diners, or other establishments frequented by travelers in the road's heyday. Staying at these lodgings allows you to connect directly with the road's past.

- Supporting Preservation Efforts: When you choose to stay at properties affiliated with Route 66 associations, you're directly supporting the preservation of the road's heritage. Revenue generated from these accommodations often goes toward maintaining historic structures, funding preservation initiatives, and promoting Route 66's continued importance.

- Cultural Immersion: These lodgings often provide an immersive cultural experience that reflects the essence of Route 66. Decor, architecture, and amenities are carefully curated to transport guests back to the road's golden era, creating a sense of nostalgia and authenticity.

- Community Involvement: Route 66 associations and their lodging properties are deeply involved in their local communities. Staying at these lodgings allows you to engage with local culture, attend events, and discover hidden gems in the towns along Route 66.

- Events and Activities: Some associations organize events and activities related to Route 66 that can enhance your stay. These may include guided tours, historical talks, classic car displays, and other activities that celebrate the road's legacy.

- Unique Accommodations: These properties offer a range of accommodations, from historic motor courts with neon signage to cozy cabins and vintage-themed rooms. You can choose the lodging that resonates most with your Route 66 adventure.

- Booking in Advance: Given their unique appeal and popularity among Route 66 enthusiasts, it's advisable to book accommodations at Route 66 association properties in advance, especially during peak travel seasons. This ensures you secure a spot at these distinctive and culturally significant lodgings.

By choosing to stay at properties affiliated with Route 66 associations, you not only enjoy a memorable and authentic lodging experience but also play a direct role in preserving the iconic heritage of the Mother Road for future generations of travelers.

9. Camping Along Route 66: For travelers who crave a deep connection with nature and the ultimate sense of freedom, camping along Route 66 provides an immersive and adventurous lodging option. Here's what you can expect when you choose camping as your accommodation choice along the Mother Road:

- Practical Campsites: Along Route 66, you'll find a range of campsites that cater to different types of campers. These can include established campgrounds with facilities like restrooms, showers, and picnic areas, as well as more remote spots for primitive camping, where you'll need to be self-sufficient.

- Scenic Settings: Camping along Route 66 allows you to wake up to breathtaking landscapes. Depending on where you choose to camp, you could be surrounded by towering forests, desert vistas, serene lakeshores, or under the star-studded desert skies.

- Freedom and Flexibility: Camping offers the ultimate freedom to create your own schedule and adventure. You can set up camp at your own pace, cook meals over an open fire, and explore the natural wonders of Route 66 on your terms.

- Cost-Effective: Camping is often a budget-friendly choice, with campsite fees typically lower than hotel or motel rates. This leaves you with more funds to allocate toward other aspects of your Route 66 journey, such as dining or attractions.

- Outdoor Activities: Camping provides the perfect gateway to outdoor activities like hiking, fishing, birdwatching, and stargazing. Many campsites are located near recreational areas, making it easy to enjoy the natural beauty and outdoor pursuits along the route.

- Local Wildlife: Depending on your camping location, you may have the opportunity to encounter local wildlife. Keep an eye out for birds, deer, and other creatures that inhabit the diverse landscapes along Route 66.

- Planning and Preparation: Camping along Route 66 requires some planning and preparation. Be sure to check ahead for campsite availability, know the regulations of the area you plan to camp in, and bring essential camping gear and supplies. Safety and Leave No Trace principles are crucial for responsible camping.

- Limited Amenities: While some established campgrounds offer amenities like restrooms and potable water, be prepared for a more rustic experience if you choose primitive camping. You'll need to bring your own water, food, and camping gear, and practice Leave No Trace principles to minimize your impact on the environment.

- Weather Considerations: Route 66's weather can vary significantly depending on the season and location. Be aware of the climate conditions in the area you plan to camp and prepare accordingly, especially for extreme temperatures.

- Booking and Availability: Established campgrounds may require reservations, especially during peak travel seasons. It's advisable to check availability and book in advance to secure a campsite, especially at popular sites.

Camping along Route 66 offers a unique blend of adventure, immersion in nature, and a true sense of freedom. Whether you're an experienced camper or new to the outdoor experience, Route 66's diverse camping options provide an opportunity to connect with the road's natural beauty and create lasting memories.

10. Luxury Accommodations Along Route 66:
For travelers seeking a touch of opulence and refinement along their Route 66 journey, upscale and luxury accommodations offer an elevated lodging experience. These accommodations are typically found in major cities along the route and provide a higher level of comfort, service, and amenities.

1. City Luxuries: Major cities along Route 66, such as Chicago, St. Louis, and Los Angeles, boast luxury hotels that cater to discerning travelers. These establishments often feature plush bedding, spa facilities, gourmet dining options, and concierge services to ensure a lavish stay.

2. Historic Grandeur: Some luxury accommodations along Route 66 are housed in historic buildings with grand architecture and rich stories. Staying in these properties offers a chance to immerse yourself in the opulence and glamour of a bygone era.

3. Fine Dining: Luxury hotels frequently have on-site restaurants that serve gourmet cuisine prepared by renowned chefs. Enjoying a sumptuous meal at these establishments can be a culinary highlight of your Route 66 adventure.

4. Spa Retreats: Pamper yourself with spa and wellness amenities available at many luxury accommodations. After a day of exploration, unwind with massages, facials, and relaxation therapies.

5. Rooftop Views: In urban luxury hotels, rooftop bars and lounges often provide stunning panoramic views of the cityscape. Sip cocktails while taking in the sights of iconic landmarks.

6. Business and Conference Facilities: For travelers mixing business with leisure, luxury accommodations often offer well-equipped meeting and conference facilities, ensuring a comfortable and productive stay.

7. Concierge Services: The attentive staff at luxury hotels can assist with arranging tours, transportation, and other services to enhance your Route 66 experience. They can also provide insider recommendations for local attractions and dining.

8. Privacy and Comfort: Luxury accommodations prioritize privacy and comfort, offering spacious rooms, high-quality linens, and premium amenities to ensure a restful night's sleep.

9. Exclusive Packages: Look for special packages and offers that may include perks like spa treatments, dining credits, or guided tours, allowing you to tailor your luxury experience.

10. Celebrity Connections: Some luxury accommodations along Route 66 have hosted celebrities and historical figures throughout the years. Staying in these iconic rooms can add an extra layer of glamour to your journey.

While luxury accommodations may be more concentrated in major urban centers along Route 66, they provide a delightful contrast to the road's nostalgic and historic side. Whether you're celebrating a special occasion or simply indulging in luxury for the night, these lodgings ensure a memorable and refined experience on the Mother Road.

Here are some examples of luxury accommodations along Route 66:

1. The Langham Huntington, Pasadena (Pasadena, California):

This historic luxury hotel in Pasadena offers elegant rooms, a beautiful pool area, and impeccable service. It's a great choice for travelers exploring the Los Angeles area.

2. The Ritz-Carlton, St. Louis (St. Louis, Missouri):

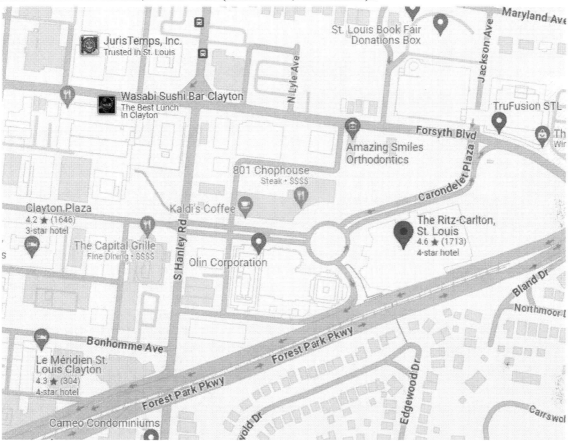

Located in Clayton, Missouri, just outside St. Louis, this Ritz-Carlton property offers luxurious rooms, a spa, and fine dining options.

3. El Tovar Hotel (Grand Canyon Village, Arizona):

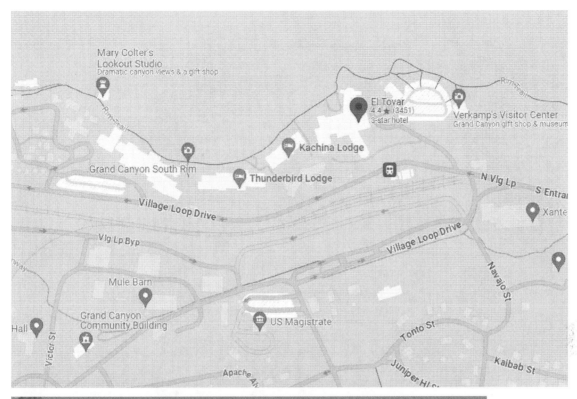

If you're planning a visit to the Grand Canyon, the El Tovar Hotel is a historic and upscale choice. It's perched right on the rim of the canyon and offers breathtaking views.

4. La Fonda on the Plaza (Santa Fe, New Mexico):

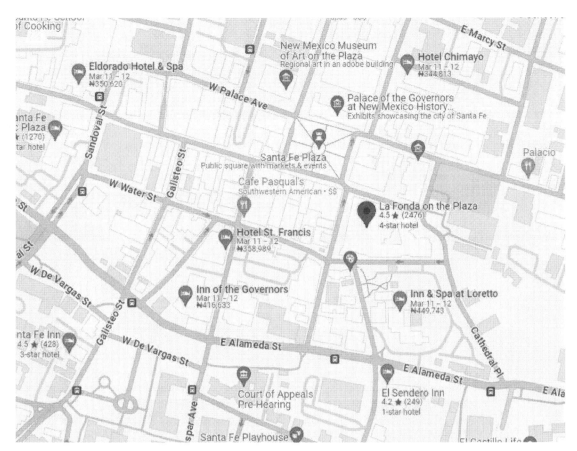

Situated in the heart of Santa Fe, this luxury hotel combines Southwestern charm with top-notch amenities. It's within walking distance of Santa Fe's historic plaza.

5. The Drake Hotel (Chicago, Illinois):

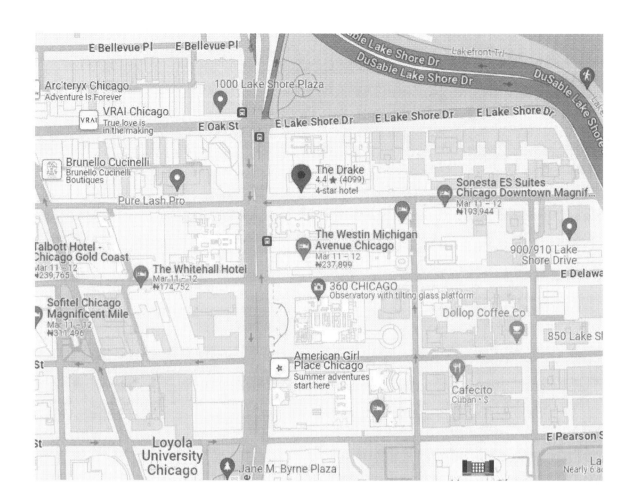

This iconic hotel in downtown Chicago is known for its elegance and history. It's a great choice for travelers starting their Route 66 journey in the Windy City.

Keep in mind that Route 66 passes through a variety of landscapes and regions, so the availability of accommodations may vary. It's advisable to plan your lodging in advance, especially during peak travel seasons, to ensure you have a comfortable place to rest each night. Whether you're seeking a retro motel experience, a cozy bed and breakfast, or a modern hotel, Route 66 offers a wide range of choices to enhance your journey.

Dining Recommendations

Dining Along Route 66:

One of the joys of traveling along Route 66 is savoring the diverse culinary experiences offered by the road's eclectic mix of diners, cafes, and restaurants. Here are dining recommendations to whet your appetite along the Mother Road:

1. Classic Diners Along Route 66:
Route 66 is synonymous with classic diners that exude a sense of nostalgic charm. These timeless establishments offer much more than just a meal; they provide a journey back in time. As you embark on your Route 66 adventure, make sure to experience the delights of these classic diners:

- Lou Mitchell's (Chicago, Illinois):

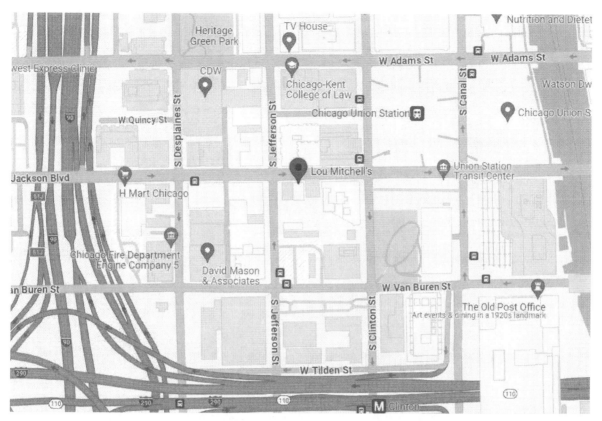

Kickstart your journey at the official starting point of Route 66 with a visit to Lou Mitchell's in Chicago. This iconic diner, which has been serving travelers since 1923, welcomes you with complimentary donut holes and orange slices. The hearty breakfast options, including fluffy pancakes and omelets, will fuel your excitement for the road ahead.

- Midpoint Cafe (Adrian, Texas):

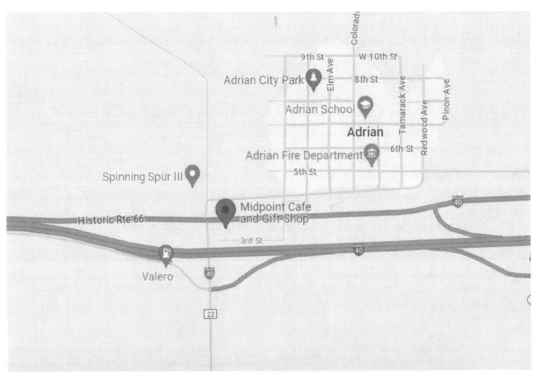

Located in Adrian, Texas, the Midpoint Cafe is not just a place to refuel your vehicle but also your appetite. As the name suggests, it's situated at the exact midpoint of Route 66, making it a must-stop for travelers. Sink your teeth into juicy burgers, savor homemade pies, and wash it all down with a classic milkshake, all while soaking in the nostalgia of this charming diner.

- Retro Atmosphere: Classic diners along Route 66 transport you to a bygone era with their retro decor, neon signage, and vintage memorabilia. The checkerboard floors, swivel stools at the counter, and jukeboxes evoke the feel of the 1950s and '60s, allowing you to dine in an ambiance steeped in history.

- All-Day Comfort Food: These diners are known for their all-day comfort food menus. Whether you're craving a hearty breakfast to start your day, a classic BLT sandwich for lunch, or a plate of meatloaf and mashed potatoes for dinner, classic diners have it all. It's a comforting and familiar culinary journey.

- Friendly Faces: Route 66 diners are often family-owned and operated, and you'll find that the staff and patrons are as welcoming as the food is satisfying. Strike up a conversation with locals and fellow travelers, and you're bound to hear fascinating stories about the road.

- Iconic Roadside Stops: Classic diners aren't just places to eat; they're iconic roadside stops where generations of travelers have refueled and created lasting memories. From the stories shared over a cup of coffee to the photos taken with vintage cars parked outside, these diners are woven into the fabric of Route 66's history.

- Milkshakes and Pies: Don't forget to indulge in some of the classic diner's signature treats. Sip on creamy milkshakes that come in a rainbow of flavors, and be sure to save room for a slice of homemade pie—apple, cherry, or pecan, the choices are as tempting as the open road itself.

- The Spirit of Route 66: Classic diners embody the spirit of Route 66—a sense of adventure, discovery, and the joy of the journey. They serve as essential waypoints where you can pause, reflect on the road ahead, and appreciate the enduring allure of the Mother Road.

So, when you travel Route 66, take the time to experience the magic of classic diners. These beloved eateries are more than places to eat; they are portals to a simpler time when the journey was as important as the destination, and every meal was a memory in the making.

2. Local Eateries Along Route 66:
One of the joys of traveling along Route 66 is the opportunity to indulge in the diverse and authentic regional cuisine found at local eateries. Each state along the Mother Road has its culinary specialties waiting to be savored. Here's a taste of what you can discover:

Oklahoma's Chicken-Fried Steak:

In the heart of Oklahoma, don't miss the chance to savor a true Southern classic—chicken-fried steak. This hearty dish features a tenderized and breaded steak, fried to golden perfection, and smothered in creamy white gravy. Local diners and restaurants along Route 66 serve up some of the best renditions of this comfort food favorite.

New Mexico's Green Chile Dishes:

New Mexico is famous for its green chile cuisine, and along Route 66, you'll find a variety of dishes featuring these flavorful peppers. Try green chile enchiladas, green chile burgers, or the iconic New Mexican green chile stew. The spicy kick of green chiles adds a unique southwestern flair to your culinary journey.

Texas Barbecue:

When you cross into Texas, you're in barbecue country, and you can't visit the Lone Star State without savoring some mouthwatering barbecue. From tender brisket and smoky ribs to savory sausages and flavorful pulled pork, Texas barbecue joints along Route 66 offer a finger-licking experience that's second to none.

Regional Favorites: Along the entire route, keep an eye out for local specialties that reflect the culture and heritage of the region. In Missouri, try toasted ravioli, a St. Louis invention, or indulge in gooey butter cake. In Arizona, sample Navajo tacos, and in California, savor seafood dishes inspired by the Pacific coast.

Homemade Pies: Route 66 is known for its charming diners and cafes that serve up homemade pies made from family recipes. Whether it's a slice of pecan pie in Oklahoma or a classic apple pie in Illinois, these sweet treats are the perfect way to end a delicious meal.

Family-Run Restaurants: Many local eateries along Route 66 are family-run and have been serving generations of travelers. These establishments offer not only great food but also a warm and welcoming atmosphere, where you can chat with locals and immerse yourself in the community's culture.

Farm-to-Table Delights: As you journey along Route 66, you may encounter farm-to-table restaurants that showcase fresh, locally sourced ingredients. These establishments often create seasonal menus that highlight the flavors of the region and support local farmers and producers.

Spicy Chili Variations: Chili is a beloved dish along Route 66, and each state adds its twist. Try Oklahoma's meaty chili served over spaghetti (known as "chili mac"), New Mexico's green or red chili stew, or Texas-style chili with a fiery kick.

Culinary Adventures: Exploring local eateries along Route 66 is not just about the food; it's about the culinary adventure and the opportunity to connect with the flavors and traditions of each region. Be open to trying something new and savoring the distinctive tastes of the road.

As you dine at these local establishments, you'll not only satisfy your taste buds but also gain a deeper appreciation for the rich and diverse culinary tapestry that Route 66 has to offer. So, embrace regional flavors and embark on a delicious journey through the heart of America.

3. Roadside Cafes Along Route 66:
Route 66 is dotted with charming roadside cafes that beckon travelers with their quirky charm and heartfelt hospitality. These establishments are more than just places to grab a meal; they are experiences infused with nostalgia and a dash of Americana. Here's a glimpse into the world of roadside cafes:

A Taste of Nostalgia: Roadside cafes along Route 66 transport you back in time with their retro decor, neon signs, and vintage memorabilia. Step inside, and you'll find checkerboard floors, cozy booths, and counters with swivel stools, creating an ambiance that evokes the spirit of the 1950s and '60s.

Homemade Pies: One of the hallmark features of roadside cafes is their dedication to the art of pie-making. These establishments take great pride in serving up slices of homemade pie in a variety of flavors. Whether it's classic apple, rich pecan, or tangy lemon meringue, the pies are often baked fresh daily and served with a dollop of nostalgia.

Comfort Food Classics: Roadside cafes are known for their all-American comfort food classics. You can expect to find dishes like meatloaf with mashed potatoes, country fried chicken, chicken and dumplings, and hearty sandwiches stacked high with fresh ingredients. These are the meals that warm the soul and satisfy the appetite of weary travelers.

Friendly Atmosphere: One of the charms of roadside cafes is the friendly and welcoming atmosphere. Many of these establishments are family-owned and operated, and the staff treats you like an old friend. It's not uncommon to strike up conversations with locals or fellow travelers, sharing stories of the road and the delights of the cafe.

Ariston Cafe (Litchfield, Illinois):

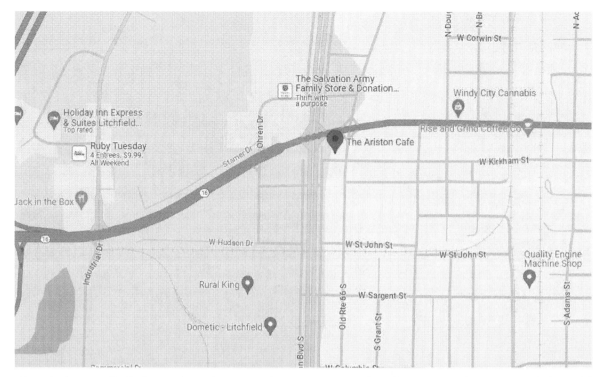

The Ariston Cafe is an iconic stop along Route 66, often touted as one of the oldest continuously operated restaurants on the route. This historic cafe has been serving classic American fare since 1924 and is a testament to the enduring appeal of roadside dining. Be sure to try their famous horseshoe sandwich, a regional specialty that features an open-faced sandwich piled high with meat, fries, and cheese.

Live Music and Entertainment: Some roadside cafes offer more than just food; they provide live music and entertainment. On certain nights, you might find local musicians strumming guitars, or even a jukebox playing your favorite tunes. It's an extra layer of enjoyment that adds to the overall experience.

Photo Opportunities: Roadside cafes often embrace their kitschy side, and you'll likely find quirky photo opportunities outside the establishment. Larger-than-life statues, vintage cars, and colorful signs provide fantastic backdrops for capturing memories of your Route 66 journey.

Community Hubs: These cafes often serve as community hubs, where locals gather for breakfast meetings, and travelers seek advice on their journey. It's a place where the past and present intersect, creating a sense of timelessness.

Collectibles and Souvenirs: Many roadside cafes have a small gift shop area filled with Route 66 memorabilia and collectibles. It's a chance to pick up a memento of your journey and support the cafe's legacy.

The Heart of Route 66: Roadside cafes are more than just places to eat; they are an integral part of the Route 66 experience. They embody the spirit of the open road, the joy of discovery, and the nostalgia of a bygone era. So, as you travel Route 66, be sure to pull over and savor a meal or a slice of pie at one of these beloved roadside cafes.

4. Ethnic Cuisine Along Route 66:
One of the remarkable aspects of traveling Route 66 is the opportunity to embark on a culinary journey that mirrors the diverse cultures and communities found along the route. From east to west, you'll encounter a vibrant melting pot of ethnic cuisine that adds a rich tapestry of flavors to your road trip experience:

☐ New Mexican Tacos: As you venture through New Mexico, be sure to indulge in the local Mexican cuisine, especially the tacos. New Mexico is renowned for its unique take on this beloved dish, featuring soft corn tortillas filled with a variety of flavorful options, often topped with red or green chile sauce. It's a taste of the Southwest that's not to be missed.

☐ Italian Pasta in Missouri: In the heart of Missouri, you can savor the flavors of Italy. Many Italian-American restaurants along Route 66 serve up classic pasta dishes like spaghetti and meatballs, fettuccine Alfredo, and lasagna. It's a comforting and hearty meal that provides a delicious contrast to the road's American classics.

☐ Vietnamese Pho in California: As you reach the western end of Route 66 in California, explore the diverse culinary scene, including Vietnamese cuisine. Pho, a fragrant and flavorful noodle soup, is a popular dish in Vietnamese restaurants along the route. It's a comforting and aromatic bowl of goodness that warms the soul.

☐ Tex-Mex Delights: In Texas, you'll encounter a fusion of Texan and Mexican flavors known as Tex-Mex cuisine. Enjoy dishes like enchiladas, chili con carne, and guacamole, often served with a side of tortilla chips and salsa. Tex-Mex is a spicy and hearty culinary adventure that reflects the Lone Star State's unique heritage.

☐ Greek Gyros in Illinois: Illinois offers a taste of Greece with its Greek gyros. These delicious wraps feature seasoned and thinly sliced meats, typically served in warm pita bread with fresh vegetables and a tangy yogurt-based tzatziki sauce. It's a Mediterranean treat that's perfect for a quick and satisfying meal.

Regional Specialties: Route 66's culinary diversity goes beyond specific ethnic cuisines. Along the way, you'll encounter regional specialties that reflect the unique cultures and traditions of each state. From Navajo tacos in Arizona to St. Louis-style toasted ravioli in Missouri, these regional dishes provide a deeper connection to the communities you visit.

International Flavors: Route 66 serves as a gateway to international flavors, offering travelers the opportunity to explore the world's cuisines without leaving the country. It's a testament to the cultural mosaic that makes America a diverse and flavorful nation.

A Culinary Adventure: Embracing ethnic cuisine along Route 66 adds a delightful layer of adventure to your journey. It allows you to not only savor new flavors but also to connect with the communities that have shaped the road's culinary landscape.

Local Favorites: When exploring ethnic cuisine, don't forget to ask locals for their recommendations. They can point you to hidden gems and family-run restaurants that offer an authentic taste of their culture.

So, as you travel Route 66, be sure to explore the diverse world of ethnic cuisine that lines the route. It's a flavorful and culturally enriching experience that adds depth to your road trip adventure.

5. Historic Landmark Dining Along Route 66:

Route 66 isn't just about the road itself; it's also about the historic landmarks and iconic dining establishments that have become an integral part of the route's lore. As you journey along the Mother Road, be sure to stop at these historic landmarks that offer not only great food but also a taste of the road's enduring legacy:

The Rock Cafe (Stroud, Oklahoma):

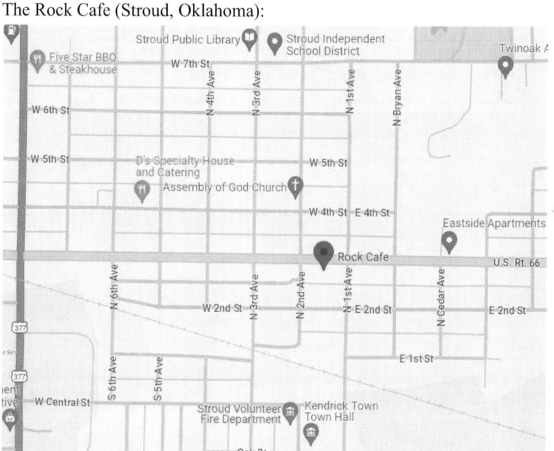

The Rock Cafe is a testament to resilience. This historic diner, built in 1939, survived not one but two fires and continues to serve travelers with its hearty American fare. What makes it truly special is its rock-solid construction – the building is made of local sandstone, giving it both character and durability. It's a place where the past meets the present, and where you can enjoy a meal infused with history.

Snow Cap Drive-In (Seligman, Arizona):

This quirky and colorful drive-in has been a Route 66 favorite since the 1950s. It's known for its playful sense of humor, with the owner often engaging in light-hearted banter with customers. Enjoy classic drive-in fare like burgers, hot dogs, and shakes while soaking in the retro atmosphere. Don't forget to try their famous "cheeseburger with cheese."

6. Farm-to-Table Dining Along Route 66:
As the culinary world evolves and embraces sustainable practices, farm-to-table dining has found its place along Route 66. Travelers now have the opportunity to savor dishes made with fresh, locally sourced ingredients that celebrate the unique flavors of the regions along the route. Here's a taste of the farm-to-table dining experience you can enjoy along Route 66:

Local Ingredients: Farm-to-table restaurants on Route 66 prioritize using ingredients sourced from nearby farms and producers. This commitment to local sourcing ensures that you're enjoying the freshest and most seasonally inspired dishes available.

Regional Flavors: One of the joys of farm-to-table dining is the celebration of regional flavors. Each stop along Route 66 offers a distinct culinary identity, whether it's the green chiles of New Mexico, the barbecue of Texas, or the Midwestern comfort foods of Illinois. Farm-to-table restaurants take these flavors and elevate them, creating dishes that are both familiar and exciting.

Menus Reflecting the Seasons: Farm-to-table restaurants often change their menus with the seasons, showcasing the bounty of each time of year. You might encounter springtime asparagus, summer heirloom tomatoes, fall squashes, and winter root vegetables, all prepared in creative and delectable ways.

Supporting Local Farmers: Dining at farm-to-table restaurants contributes to the sustainability of local farming communities. These establishments prioritize purchasing from nearby farms, helping to strengthen the local food economy and reduce the carbon footprint associated with food transportation.

Fresh and Vibrant Salads: Farm-to-table dining often features vibrant and fresh salads that showcase the best of local produce. From crisp lettuce to colorful vegetables and homemade dressings, these salads are a healthy and delicious option.

Craft Beverages: Many farm-to-table restaurants also emphasize craft beverages, such as locally brewed beers, wines, and artisanal cocktails. These pair perfectly with your farm-fresh meal, adding an extra layer of enjoyment to your dining experience.

Cozy Atmosphere: Farm-to-table restaurants on Route 66 often feature cozy and welcoming atmospheres. Whether it's a historic building, a charming cottage, or a rustic barn, these dining establishments provide a relaxed and enjoyable environment to savor your meal.

Culinary Creativity: Chefs at farm-to-table restaurants along Route 66 take pride in their culinary creativity. They often experiment with unique combinations of local ingredients to create memorable and one-of-a-kind dishes that reflect the essence of the region.

Community Connection: Farm-to-table dining fosters a sense of community connection. You'll find that many of these restaurants have close relationships with local farmers and producers, and they may even host events that celebrate local food and culture.

So, as you travel along Route 66, keep an eye out for farm-to-table dining options. They provide an opportunity to not only enjoy delicious and fresh cuisine but also to support the local food ecosystem and experience the unique flavors of each region along the route. It's a culinary journey that celebrates sustainability, seasonality, and the rich agricultural traditions of America's Main Street.

7. Barbecue Joints Along Route 66:
One of the joys of traveling Route 66 is indulging in the diverse and delicious world of barbecue. As you journey along the route, you'll have the opportunity to sample some of the nation's finest barbecue dishes, each with its own regional twist. Here are some barbecue joints that should be on your list:

Pappy's Smokehouse (St. Louis, Missouri):

Pappy's is a St. Louis institution known for its mouthwatering ribs. The succulent, slow-smoked ribs are so tender they practically fall off the bone. Pair them with classic sides like baked beans and coleslaw for the ultimate barbecue experience.

Joe's Kansas City Bar-B-Que (Kansas City, Kansas):

When it comes to barbecue, Kansas City is legendary, and Joe's is a must-visit destination. Their Z-Man sandwich, featuring sliced brisket, provolone cheese, onion rings, and barbecue sauce on a Kaiser roll, is a fan favorite. Don't forget to try the burnt ends—a true Kansas City specialty.

Barbecue Varieties: Along Route 66, you'll encounter a variety of barbecue styles, from the sweet and tangy sauces of Kansas City to the smoky and spicy flavors of

Texas. Each region has its unique take on barbecue, offering a delicious exploration of the country's culinary diversity.

Barbecue Traditions: Barbecue is more than just a meal; it's a tradition and a way of life in many communities along Route 66. These barbecue joints often have a rich history and a loyal following, making them integral parts of the road's culture.

Local Flavors: Don't forget to explore local barbecue joints in smaller towns and cities along the route. These hidden gems often serve up authentic regional flavors and provide a chance to connect with locals and fellow travelers over a shared love for barbecue.

So, whether you're a barbecue connoisseur or just a lover of good food, Route 66 offers a tantalizing journey through the world of barbecue. Be sure to savor the smoky, savory, and saucy delights that await you at these iconic barbecue joints.

8. Route 66-Themed Restaurants:
As you travel along Route 66, you'll encounter a unique breed of restaurants that go beyond just serving delicious food. These eateries pay homage to Route 66's rich history and culture, offering diners a journey back in time and a taste of the road's enduring spirit. Here are some Route 66-themed restaurants that add an extra layer of nostalgia to your dining experience:

Route 66 Drive-In Theater and Restaurant (Webb City, Missouri):

This establishment is a true gem along the route, combining the best of classic cars, movies, and great food. The Route 66 Drive-In Theater and Restaurant takes you on a trip down memory lane with its vintage car-themed decor and drive-in movie experience. Enjoy a meal in your car or at a picnic table while watching a classic film on the big screen. It's an immersive blast from the past that captures the essence of Route 66's heyday.

Delgadillo's Snow Cap in Seligman is not only a quirky roadside diner but also a whimsical experience. The restaurant is known for its playful sense of humor, and the menu includes items like the "cheeseburger with cheese" and "dead chicken." The exterior is adorned with colorful, eye-catching signs and decorations, making it a must-stop for those seeking a fun and lighthearted Route 66 encounter.

Cozy Dog Drive-In (Springfield, Illinois):

For those who want to sample Route 66's culinary history, the Cozy Dog Drive-In in Springfield is a must-visit. This nostalgic spot is credited with inventing the famous "corn dog on a stick." Step back in time and savor this classic American snack in a setting that harks back to the golden era of drive-ins.

Emma Jean's Holland Burger Cafe (Victorville, California):

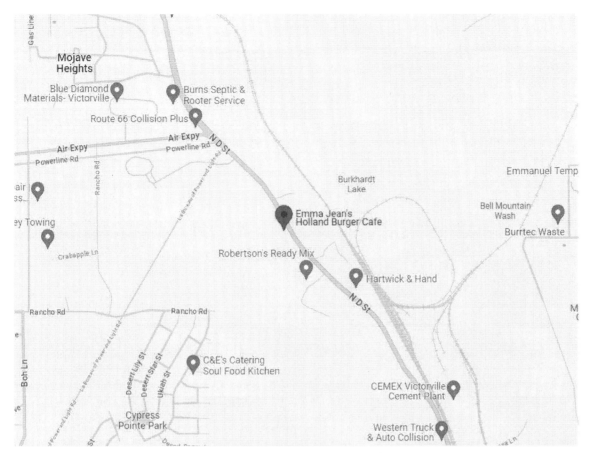

Emma Jean's is a beloved Route 66 institution known for its vintage charm and mouth watering burgers. The cafe's retro atmosphere and friendly service make it a welcoming stop for travelers looking to experience the nostalgia of the road.

Unique Atmospheres: Route 66-themed restaurants often go the extra mile to create unique atmospheres that transport diners to a bygone era. The decor, signage, and even the staff's attire contribute to the overall immersive experience.

Roadside Adventure: These eateries add an element of adventure to your journey. They are not just places to eat but destinations that evoke the spirit of exploration and discovery that Route 66 is known for.

So, as you dine along Route 66, be sure to seek out these themed restaurants that embrace the road's history and culture. They provide not only memorable meals but also an opportunity to step back in time and relive the magic of America's Main Street.

9. Bakeries and Sweet Treats Along Route 66:
Route 66 isn't just about savory delights; it also has a sweet side waiting to be explored. Along the road, you'll find charming bakeries and sweet shops that tempt travelers with homemade pies, donuts, pastries, and other delectable treats. Here are some sweet spots to satisfy your cravings:

Pops on Route 66 (Arcadia, Oklahoma):

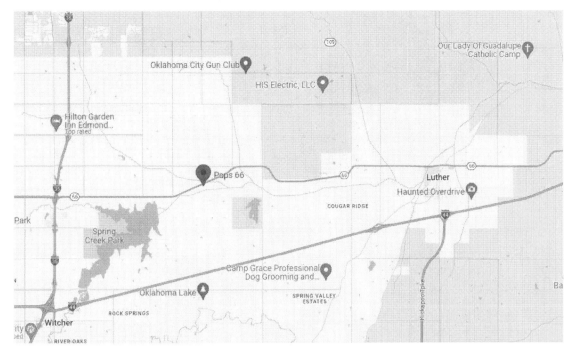

Pops is a must-visit destination for those with a sweet tooth and a love for all things fizzy. While primarily known for its extensive soda selection, Pops also offers a tempting assortment of ice creams and sweets. Try a float with your favorite soda paired with a scoop of ice cream for a delightful treat.

Bagdad Cafe (Newberry Springs, California):

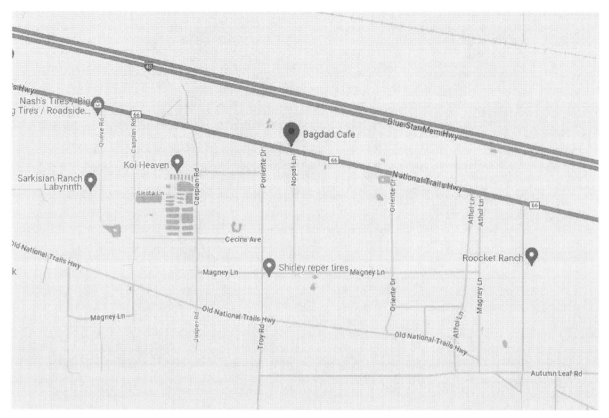

The Bagdad Cafe isn't just a place for a meal; it's also known for its delicious pies and pastries. After enjoying a meal at this quirky Route 66 landmark, treat yourself to a slice of pie or a sweet dessert to cap off your visit.

So, as you journey along Route 66, be sure to indulge your sweet tooth with the delightful offerings of bakeries and sweet shops. Whether you're craving a classic American pie or a unique dessert creation, you'll find a wide variety of sweet treats to make your road trip even sweeter.

10. Food Festivals Along Route 66:
One of the joys of traveling Route 66 is the opportunity to immerse yourself in the diverse culinary traditions of the regions it crosses. Food festivals along the route celebrate local flavors, offering a vibrant tapestry of tastes and experiences. Here are some food festivals you might want to plan your journey around:

Albuquerque International Balloon Fiesta (Albuquerque, New Mexico):

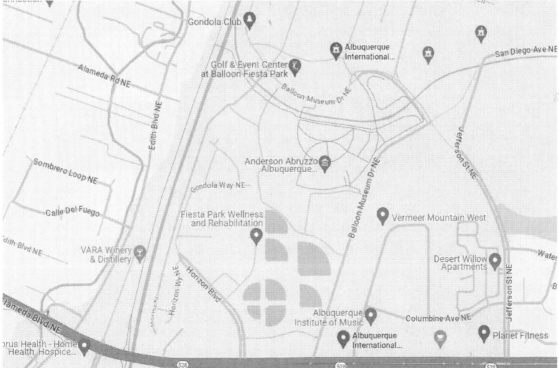

While renowned for its stunning hot air balloons, the Albuquerque International Balloon Fiesta also boasts a diverse array of food vendors. From traditional New

Mexican dishes like green chile stew to international cuisine, the festival offers a culinary adventure to complement the visual spectacle.

Rockabilly on the Route (Tucumcari, New Mexico): This music and vintage car festival in Tucumcari is a celebration of all things retro, including classic diner fare. Enjoy burgers, fries, and shakes while grooving to rock 'n' roll tunes and admiring the impressive display of vintage automobiles.

11. Dining with a View Along Route 66:
One of the unique pleasures of traveling Route 66 is the opportunity to savor a delicious meal while taking in breathtaking views of natural wonders. These restaurants not only offer scrumptious cuisine but also a visual feast of stunning landscapes. Here's a notable spot for dining with a view:

Top of the Rock Restaurant (Ridgedale, Missouri): Perched atop a bluff overlooking the serene Table Rock Lake, the Top of the Rock Restaurant provides a dining experience like no other. Whether you're enjoying a leisurely brunch or a romantic dinner, the panoramic views of the lake and the Ozark Mountains create an unforgettable backdrop. It's the perfect setting for savoring a meal while immersing yourself in the beauty of the Missouri wilderness.

A Feast for the Senses: Restaurants like the Top of the Rock not only treat your taste buds but also offer a feast for your eyes. The combination of delectable dishes and stunning vistas elevates your dining experience to new heights.

Romantic Getaway: If you're traveling with a loved one, these restaurants with a view provide a romantic ambiance that's perfect for celebrating special moments along the Mother Road.

Scenic Drives: Many of these dining spots are situated along scenic byways, making the journey to the restaurant as enjoyable as the meal itself. You'll find yourself winding through picturesque landscapes en route to your culinary destination.

When you're planning your Route 66 adventure, consider incorporating a stop at a restaurant that offers a dining experience enhanced by the beauty of nature. Whether you're looking for a romantic evening or simply want to enjoy a meal with a view, these restaurants add an extra layer of wonder to your journey down America's Main Street.

12. Local Breweries and Wineries Along Route 66:
As you travel along Route 66, don't miss the opportunity to explore the vibrant craft beer and wine scene that has blossomed in various regions. Local breweries and wineries offer a taste of the area's unique flavors and a chance to raise a glass to your journey. Here are some notable stops for craft beer and wine enthusiasts:

St. James Winery (St. James, Missouri):

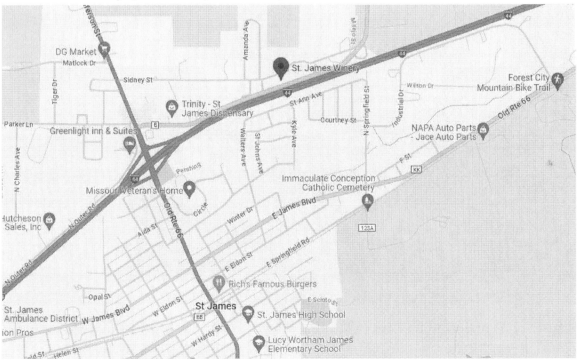

Known as the "Meramec Highlands," this region boasts vineyards and wineries. St. James Winery, in particular, offers a delightful selection of award-winning Missouri wines. Take a winery tour and indulge in wine tastings to discover the flavors of the Ozarks.

Desert Diamond Distillery (Kingman, Arizona):

For those who appreciate spirits, Desert Diamond Distillery in Kingman produces artisanal rum, vodka, and other libations. Join a distillery tour to learn about the distillation process and enjoy tastings of their handcrafted products.

Local Flavors: Breweries and wineries often showcase local ingredients, giving you a taste of the terroir and the unique character of the region.

Craftsmanship: These establishments are typically passionate about their craft, offering a chance to meet the brewers or vintners and gain insights into the art of brewing and winemaking.

Community Gathering: Breweries, in particular, have become community hubs where locals and travelers alike gather to share stories and experiences.

Pairing Opportunities: Consider pairing local beers or wines with regional cuisine for a complete culinary experience.

Whether you're a wine connoisseur, a craft beer enthusiast, or simply someone who enjoys sipping on quality beverages, Route 66 offers a variety of options to satisfy your palate. So, as you journey down the highway, raise a glass to the flavors of the road and the memories you're creating along the way.

RV Parks and Camping Sites

For travelers who prefer the freedom and adventure of RV camping, Route 66 offers a wide range of RV parks and camping sites that cater to various preferences and needs. Here are some notable options along the route:

Grand Canyon RV Glamping (Williams, Arizona):

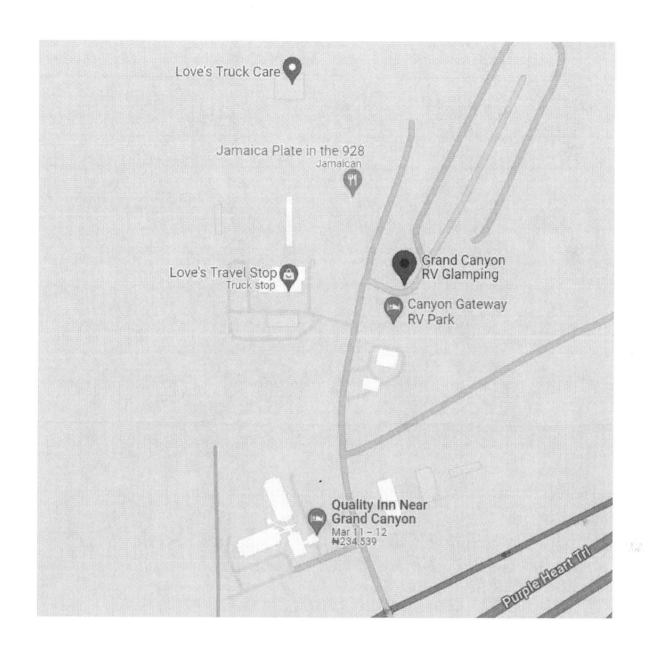

If you're seeking an extraordinary camping experience near the world-famous Grand Canyon, the Grand Canyon RV Glamping site in Williams, Arizona, offers a distinctive blend of luxury and adventure. This isn't your typical RV camping; it's RV glamping, where you can enjoy the great outdoors without sacrificing comfort and style.

- Luxury RVs: At this glamping site, you'll find a selection of luxurious RVs that are thoughtfully designed to provide a premium camping experience. These RVs often include private bathrooms, fully equipped kitchens, comfortable sleeping areas, and stylish interiors.

- Comfort Amid Nature: While you'll be in the heart of nature, surrounded by the breathtaking beauty of the Grand Canyon region, you won't have to forgo modern comforts. Enjoy a hot shower in your private bathroom, whip up a delicious meal in the well-equipped kitchen, and relax in a cozy living area after a day of exploration.

- Scenic Setting: Williams, Arizona, serves as an ideal base for visiting the Grand Canyon, and this RV glamping site ensures you're immersed in the natural splendor of the area. Wake up to scenic views, step outside to breathe in the crisp mountain air, and savor the ambiance of camping under the stars.

- Convenience: RV glamping provides the convenience of RV travel without the need to own or rent your own RV. Everything you need for a comfortable stay is already in place, allowing you to focus on enjoying the Grand Canyon and its surroundings.

- Unique Experience: Glamping at the Grand Canyon offers a unique blend of adventure and luxury, allowing you to create lasting memories in one of the most iconic natural landscapes in the world.

For travelers who want to experience the grandeur of the Grand Canyon without sacrificing the comforts of home, Grand Canyon RV Glamping in Williams, Arizona, offers an exceptional solution. It's a stylish and convenient way to explore one of nature's most awe-inspiring wonders while enjoying the modern amenities of RV glamping.

Jellystone Park at Route 66 (Eureka, Missouri):

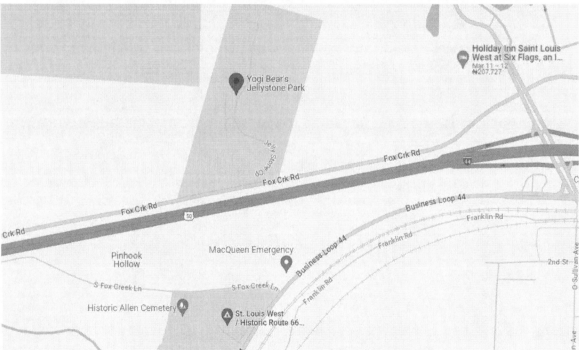

For families embarking on a Route 66 adventure, the Jellystone Park at Route 66 in Eureka, Missouri, is a haven of fun and entertainment. This RV camping destination is tailored to provide a memorable experience for both children and those young at heart.

- Family-Friendly Activities: Jellystone Park is renowned for its family-oriented activities and amenities. From water slides and mini-golf to swimming pools and playgrounds, there's no shortage of ways to keep the kids entertained and ensure they have a blast.

- Themed Weekends: The park often hosts themed weekends and special events, adding an extra layer of excitement to your stay. Whether it's a themed costume contest, a campfire sing-along, or a holiday celebration, these events create lasting memories for families.

- Social Atmosphere: Jellystone Park is designed to encourage social interaction among campers. It's a place where families can connect with other travelers, share stories around the campfire, and create a sense of community.

- Amenities: In addition to the fun-filled activities, you'll find practical amenities like laundry facilities, Wi-Fi, and camp stores, ensuring you have everything you need during your stay.

- Convenient Location: Located in Eureka, Missouri, Jellystone Park is well-positioned for exploring Route 66 attractions in the area. After a day of adventure, you can return to the park for a relaxing evening of family-friendly entertainment.

- Memorable Experiences: Whether it's a thrilling ride down a water slide or a themed weekend full of laughter, Jellystone Park is all about creating cherished moments that your family will treasure for years to come.

For families traveling along Route 66, Jellystone Park at Route 66 in Eureka, Missouri, offers a delightful combination of outdoor adventure and family-friendly entertainment. It's a place where kids can be kids, and parents can relish in the joy of watching their little adventurers explore and play.

Elk City/Clinton KOA Journey (Elk City, Oklahoma):

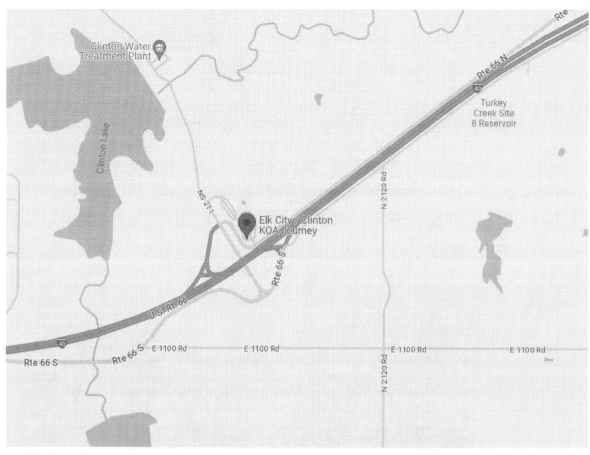

For travelers seeking a comfortable and family-friendly RV camping experience near Route 66, the Elk City/Clinton KOA Journey in Elk City, Oklahoma, offers a welcoming oasis. KOA (Kampgrounds of America) locations are known for their well-maintained facilities and commitment to providing a fantastic camping experience.

- Convenient Location: This KOA is strategically positioned for travelers exploring Route 66 attractions in the region. It provides easy access to the iconic highway and its myriad of landmarks and points of interest.

- Amenities: KOA campgrounds are renowned for their amenities, and Elk City/Clinton KOA Journey is no exception. You'll find facilities like a swimming pool, a dog park, and clean restroom and shower facilities to enhance your stay.

- Family-Friendly Atmosphere: KOA campgrounds are designed to be family-friendly, making them an excellent choice for those traveling with children. The friendly and social atmosphere often encourages kids to make new friends and enjoy the outdoors.

- Well-Maintained Sites: KOA is known for its commitment to maintaining clean and well-kept RV sites. You can expect level sites with reliable hook-ups, ensuring a hassle-free camping experience.

- Variety of Accommodations: In addition to RV sites, KOA campgrounds typically offer a variety of accommodations, including cabins and tent sites, accommodating a range of camping preferences.

- Community Vibes: KOA campgrounds often host communal activities, from pancake breakfasts to campfire gatherings, fostering a sense of community among travelers.

- Pet-Friendly: If you're traveling with furry companions, you'll appreciate the dog-friendly amenities like dog parks that many KOA campgrounds provide.

For RV travelers along Route 66 who value well-maintained facilities, family-friendly environments, and a convenient base for exploring the iconic highway, the Elk City/Clinton KOA Journey in Elk City, Oklahoma, offers all of these advantages. It's a place where you can relax, connect with fellow travelers, and create memorable moments during your Route 66 journey.

Route 66 RV Resort (Albuquerque, New Mexico):

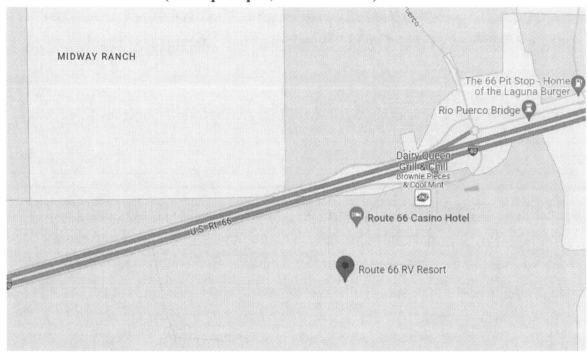

If you're seeking a modern and comfortable RV resort experience along Route 66, the Route 66 RV Resort in Albuquerque, New Mexico, combines the best of both worlds. This resort offers a blend of modern amenities and a Route 66 theme, creating an ideal base for exploring the vibrant city of Albuquerque and the surrounding attractions.

- Modern Comforts: The Route 66 RV Resort is designed to provide RV travelers with all the modern comforts they desire. This includes spacious RV sites with full hook-ups, ensuring you have everything you need for a convenient and enjoyable stay.

- Fitness Center: For those who like to stay active while on the road, the resort features a fitness center where you can maintain your workout routine, keeping you energized for your Route 66 adventures.

- Clubhouse: The clubhouse is a hub of activity at the resort, providing a place for socializing, relaxation, and entertainment. You can connect with fellow travelers, enjoy game nights, or simply unwind in a welcoming atmosphere.

- Route 66 Theme: Embracing the spirit of Route 66, the resort incorporates elements of the iconic highway into its design and ambiance. It's a place where you can immerse yourself in the history and culture of the Mother Road while enjoying modern amenities.

- Albuquerque Exploration: Located in Albuquerque, the resort offers easy access to the city's attractions, including the historic Old Town, vibrant arts scenes, and the stunning Sandia Mountains.

- Convenient Services: The Route 66 RV Resort understands the needs of RV travelers and provides essential services like laundry facilities, clean restrooms, and reliable Wi-Fi to ensure a comfortable stay.

- Outdoor Recreation: Beyond Albuquerque, you'll find a wealth of outdoor adventures, from hiking and biking in the nearby Sandia Mountains to exploring the beauty of the Rio Grande Valley.

For RV enthusiasts who appreciate modern comforts, a touch of Route 66 nostalgia, and a prime location for exploring Albuquerque and its surroundings, the Route 66 RV Resort in Albuquerque, New Mexico, offers an appealing blend of convenience and relaxation. It's a place where you can experience the best of both worlds during your Route 66 journey.

National Forest Campgrounds: For travelers who seek a closer connection with nature and a more rustic camping experience during their Route 66 journey, the national forest campgrounds along the way provide a perfect retreat. These campgrounds are nestled within pristine natural settings, offering a tranquil escape from the hustle and bustle of the highway.

- Scenic Beauty: National forest campgrounds are often located in some of the most scenic and breathtaking parts of the country. Surrounded by lush forests, serene lakes, and majestic mountains, these campgrounds provide a front-row seat to the beauty of the great outdoors.

- Outdoor Activities: If you're an outdoor enthusiast, you'll find a wealth of activities at your doorstep. Hiking, fishing, birdwatching, and stargazing are just a few of the recreational opportunities that await you in these natural settings.

- Wildlife Encounters: National forests are teeming with wildlife, and camping in these areas increases your chances of encountering native animals in their natural habitat. Keep your camera ready for potential wildlife sightings.

- Rustic Camping: While national forest campgrounds provide essential amenities like picnic tables, fire rings, and vault toilets, they typically offer a more rustic camping experience compared to RV parks and resorts. It's a chance to disconnect and enjoy the simple pleasures of camping.

- No Hook-Ups: It's important to note that most national forest campgrounds do not offer RV hook-ups, making them better suited for tent camping or RVs with self-contained systems. Be prepared to rely on your RV's resources.

- Quiet Retreat: These campgrounds tend to be quieter and less crowded than commercial RV parks, making them an ideal choice for those who value solitude and a deep connection with nature.

- Reservations: Some national forest campgrounds accept reservations, while others operate on a first-come, first-served basis. It's a good idea to check availability and make reservations if possible, especially during peak seasons.

- Leave No Trace: When camping in national forests, it's essential to follow Leave No Trace principles, which promote responsible outdoor ethics to protect the environment. This includes packing out all trash, respecting wildlife, and staying on designated trails.

For travelers who cherish the serenity of natural landscapes and seek a camping experience that immerses them in the heart of America's wilderness, national forest campgrounds along Route 66 offer the perfect retreat. It's an opportunity to connect with the great outdoors and experience the beauty and tranquility of the country's national forests.

Reservations: When planning your Route 66 journey and considering accommodations at RV parks and campgrounds, one crucial aspect to keep in mind is the option of making reservations. Reservations are particularly valuable, especially when traveling during peak travel seasons or when you have a specific destination in mind.

- Peak Travel Seasons: Route 66, being an iconic American highway, experiences periods of heightened travel activity, especially during the summer months. Many travelers embark on their Route 66 adventures during this time, which can lead to increased demand for RV park and campground spaces. Reserving a spot in advance helps secure your place during these busy times.

- Peace of Mind: Making reservations provides peace of mind. You won't need to worry about arriving at a fully booked RV park or campground after a long day on the road. Knowing that your spot is reserved allows you to focus on enjoying your journey without concerns about finding a place to stay.

- Specific Destinations: If you have specific destinations or RV parks in mind that you don't want to miss, reservations are often the best way to ensure you can stay at your desired location. This is especially true for renowned RV parks or those with limited capacity.

- Variability: Keep in mind that not all RV parks and campgrounds along Route 66 operate the same way. While some facilities readily accept reservations, others may primarily operate on a first-come, first-served basis. It's essential to research and understand the booking policies of the specific places you plan to stay.

- Booking Platforms: Many RV parks and campgrounds offer online reservation systems, making it convenient to secure your spot well in advance of your arrival date. Utilizing these platforms can streamline the reservation process.

- Flexibility: While reservations offer security, it's also wise to maintain some flexibility in your itinerary. Unexpected changes or discoveries along the road might lead you to adjust your plans. Having a mix of reserved and non-reserved stays allows for spontaneity while ensuring you have a place to rest when needed.

- Cancellation Policies: Be sure to review the cancellation policies of RV parks and campgrounds when making reservations. Understanding these policies can help you plan accordingly in case your travel plans change.

Amenities: When selecting RV parks and campgrounds along Route 66 for your journey, taking a close look at the available amenities is a key factor in ensuring a comfortable and enjoyable stay. Each traveler's preferences may differ, so it's important to consider what amenities are most important to you and your travel companions. Here are some common amenities to think about:

- Full Hook-Ups: Full hook-ups typically include water, electricity, and sewer connections for your RV. This level of service ensures you have access to essential utilities during your stay, making it convenient for longer trips.

- Wi-Fi and Connectivity: If staying connected to the internet is crucial for work, communication, or entertainment, RV parks with Wi-Fi or reliable cell phone signal may be a priority. Check if the park offers Wi-Fi access and inquire about its reliability.

- Laundry Facilities: For extended road trips, having access to laundry facilities can be a significant convenience. Look for RV parks that offer on-site laundry services so you can refresh your clothing during your journey.

- Restrooms and Showers: Clean and well-maintained restroom and shower facilities are essential for comfort during your travels. Check if the RV park provides these amenities and if they meet your standards.

- Recreational Activities: Depending on your interests, you might seek RV parks with recreational activities such as swimming pools, hiking trails, playgrounds, or game rooms. These amenities can add extra enjoyment to your stay.

- Pet-Friendly Facilities: If you're traveling with pets, ensure that the RV park is pet-friendly and offers amenities like dog parks or walking areas.

- Dump Stations: Even if you have full hook-ups, it's helpful to have access to a dump station for emptying your RV's holding tanks before hitting the road again.

- Proximity to Attractions: Consider the location of the RV park in relation to the Route 66 attractions you plan to visit. Being close to points of interest can save you travel time and make sightseeing more convenient.

- Safety and Security: Check if the RV park has security measures in place, such as well-lit areas, surveillance cameras, or gated access, to ensure the safety of your RV and belongings.

- Accessibility: Ensure that the RV park's amenities are accessible to your specific needs, whether you have mobility challenges or require ADA-compliant facilities.

- Quiet and Serene Settings: If you value peace and quiet, look for RV parks that are situated in serene and natural settings away from noise and distractions.

- Community and Social Activities: Some RV parks organize community events and social activities, providing opportunities to connect with fellow travelers.

- Cost: While not an amenity per se, the cost of staying at an RV park or campground is an important consideration. Determine if the park's amenities align with the price you're willing to pay for your stay.

Ultimately, the selection of RV parks and campgrounds should align with your preferences and needs, whether you prioritize full hook-ups, connectivity, recreational options, or a peaceful atmosphere. By carefully evaluating the amenities offered by each location, you can make informed decisions that enhance your Route 66 journey.

Scenic Beauty: One of the delightful aspects of traveling along Route 66 is the opportunity to immerse yourself in the scenic beauty of the American landscape. Many campgrounds and RV parks along this historic route are strategically located in picturesque settings, providing travelers with the chance to revel in the natural splendor of various regions. Here's why considering the scenic beauty of these locations is crucial:

- Nature's Tranquility: Campgrounds set amidst scenic beauty offer a serene and peaceful environment where you can unwind and connect with nature. The tranquil surroundings can enhance your camping experience, allowing you to relax and recharge.

- Spectacular Views: Whether it's the rugged beauty of the southwestern desert, the rolling hills of the Midwest, or the lush forests of the Pacific Northwest, scenic campgrounds often come with breathtaking views. Waking up to a stunning sunrise over a mountain range or enjoying a campfire under a starlit sky can be unforgettable moments.

- Outdoor Activities: Campgrounds in scenic areas are often surrounded by opportunities for outdoor activities such as hiking, fishing, birdwatching, and photography. The natural surroundings invite you to explore and engage in recreational pursuits that are unique to each region.

- Photographic Opportunities: If you're a photography enthusiast, staying in campgrounds with scenic beauty can provide an abundance of photographic subjects. Capture the landscape, wildlife, and changing seasons as you document your Route 66 journey.

- Disconnect and Reconnect: Scenic campgrounds can be the ideal places to disconnect from the hustle and bustle of daily life and reconnect with the natural world. Take a break from screens and city noise and bask in the sights and sounds of the great outdoors.

- Seasonal Changes: Depending on the time of year, you may witness seasonal changes in the landscape, from vibrant fall foliage to blooming wildflowers in the spring. Staying in campgrounds with scenic beauty allows you to experience these natural transformations.

- Environmental Awareness: Camping in beautiful natural settings often fosters a greater appreciation for the environment and encourages responsible and sustainable practices, such as Leave No Trace principles.

- Privacy and Solitude: Scenic campgrounds can offer a sense of privacy and solitude, allowing you to enjoy a more secluded camping experience away from the crowds.

- Stress Reduction: The calming effect of natural beauty can reduce stress and promote mental well-being. Camping in scenic locations provides an opportunity to de-stress and rejuvenate.

When planning your Route 66 journey and selecting campgrounds and RV parks, consider the scenic beauty of the locations you'll encounter along the way. Whether you prefer desert vistas, forested landscapes, or riverside views, the scenic campgrounds along Route 66 can add a touch of natural wonder to your adventure, making it an even more memorable experience.

Whether you're seeking a family-friendly RV park with entertainment options or a secluded campground to connect with nature, Route 66 accommodates a wide range of camping preferences. As you plan your journey, be sure to check the availability and amenities of the RV parks and campgrounds along your route to ensure a comfortable and memorable camping experience.

Chapter 6: Roadside Americana

Roadside Americana: Route 66, often referred to as the "Main Street of America," isn't just a historic highway; it's a journey through the heart of American culture and nostalgia. Along this iconic route, you'll encounter a captivating world of roadside Americana, where time-honored diners, neon-lit motels, quirky attractions, and vintage signs beckon travelers to step back in time. This chapter is your guide to exploring the enchanting and often whimsical side of Route 66, where every stop tells a story and every mile is a testament to the enduring spirit of the open road. So, fasten your seatbelt and get ready to dive into the colorful and unforgettable world of Roadside Americana along Route 66.

Classic Diners and Motels

When it comes to experiencing the authentic charm of Route 66, few places capture the essence of this historic highway like classic diners and motels. These iconic establishments are more than just places to eat and sleep; they're time capsules that transport you to the golden era of American road travel.

1. Nostalgia on the Menu: Classic diners along Route 66 serve up nostalgia with every plate. Step inside and you'll find retro décor, checkerboard floors, and booths that harken back to the 1950s. The menus are filled with timeless comfort foods like juicy hamburgers, thick milkshakes, and hearty breakfasts. Lou Mitchell's in Chicago and the Midpoint Cafe in Adrian, Texas, are prime examples of diners that capture this vintage spirit.

2. Neon-Lit Motels: Route 66 is renowned for its neon-lit motels that beckon weary travelers with their glowing signs. These motels often feature unique architectural designs, from wigwam-shaped rooms to classic motor court layouts. Staying in one of these motels is like taking a step back in time to an era when the open road held endless possibilities. The Blue Swallow Motel in Tucumcari, New Mexico, and the Munger Moss Motel in Lebanon, Missouri, are cherished examples of such accommodations.

3. Personalized Service: What sets classic diners and motels apart is the personalized service you'll receive. Many of these establishments are family-owned, and the owners take pride in ensuring guests have an unforgettable experience. You're not just a customer; you're part of the family.

4. Capturing the Route 66 Spirit: Classic diners and motels are not just places to stop for sustenance or rest; they embody the spirit of Route 66 itself. The neon signs, vintage cars in the parking lots, and the sense of community among fellow travelers create an atmosphere that celebrates the freedom and adventure of the open road.

5. Preservation of History: Supporting these establishments contributes to the preservation of Route 66's history. Many classic diners and motels have faced challenges over the years due to changing travel trends and modernization. By patronizing them, you play a role in keeping Route 66's iconic past alive.

In your journey along Route 66, make it a point to savor a meal at a classic diner and spend a night at a neon-lit motel. These experiences are not just about the food and lodging; they're about connecting with the heart and soul of the Mother Road, where every booth and room tells a story of adventure and nostalgia.

Vintage Gas Stations and Neon Signs

Along the historic Route 66, you'll encounter a mesmerizing world of vintage gas stations and neon signs that harken back to a bygone era of American road travel. These iconic landmarks are more than just places to refuel your vehicle; they're vibrant symbols of the spirit of the open road.

1. Gas Stations of Yesteryear: Route 66 is dotted with gas stations that transport you to a time when service attendants in uniforms filled your tank, checked your oil, and cleaned your windshield with a smile. Some of these stations have been preserved as museums, offering a glimpse into the history of motoring. Notable stops include the Texaco Station in Shamrock, Texas, and the Ambler's Texaco Gas Station in Dwight, Illinois.

2. Neon Dreams: The neon signs along Route 66 are a mesmerizing sight, especially as the sun sets and the highway comes alive with vibrant colors. These signs are works of art in their own right, with intricate designs and nostalgic imagery. Iconic examples include the Blue Whale in Catoosa, Oklahoma, and the iconic Gateway Arch in St. Louis, Missouri.

3. Timeless Appeal: Vintage gas stations and neon signs have a timeless appeal that resonates with travelers of all ages. They evoke a sense of nostalgia for a simpler time when road trips were an adventure in themselves. They're also a testament to the enduring allure of Route 66, drawing photographers, artists, and history enthusiasts from around the world.

4. Stories of the Road: Each gas station and neon sign along Route 66 has its own story to tell. Some have witnessed the journey of famous travelers, while others have weathered decades of changing travel trends. These landmarks are more than just structures; they're keepers of the road's history.

5. Preservation Efforts: Many organizations and communities along Route 66 are dedicated to the preservation of these vintage gas stations and neon signs. Their efforts ensure that future generations can continue to enjoy these iconic symbols of Americana.

As you travel along Route 66, take the time to appreciate the vintage gas stations and neon signs that line the route. They not only add to the visual spectacle of your journey but also connect you to the rich history and enduring charm of the Mother Road. Whether you're a history buff, a photography enthusiast, or simply a traveler seeking adventure, these landmarks are sure to leave a lasting impression on your Route 66 experience.

Quirky Roadside Attractions

A journey along Route 66 is more than just a drive; it's an adventure filled with quirky roadside attractions that add a dose of whimsy and wonder to your travel experience. These offbeat stops are the unexpected gems that make the Mother Road truly unforgettable.

1. World's Largest This and That: Along Route 66, you'll encounter towns vying for the title of having the "world's largest" something. Whether it's a giant rocking chair in Fanning, Missouri, or a towering ketchup bottle in Collinsville, Illinois, these oversized wonders invite you to take a photo and marvel at human creativity.

2. Muffler Men and Giant Statues: Keep an eye out for the iconic Muffler Men, towering fiberglass figures that take on various forms, from lumberjacks to cowboys. You'll also come across giant statues like the Gemini Giant in Wilmington, Illinois, and the Blue Whale in Catoosa, Oklahoma, each with its own unique story.

3. Roadside Art Installations: Route 66 is a canvas for artistic expression. From the Cadillac Ranch in Amarillo, Texas, where cars are buried nose-first in the ground, to the Bottle Tree Ranch in Oro Grande, California, where thousands of bottles create a shimmering forest, these installations blur the lines between art and roadside oddity.

4. Odd Museums: Quirky museums line the route, offering a glimpse into the eccentric and fascinating. Explore the Museum of the American Quilter in Paducah, Kentucky, or the International Banana Museum in Mecca, California, and discover collections you won't find anywhere else.

5. Unusual Architecture: Route 66 boasts its fair share of buildings with unconventional designs. The Wigwam Motels, with their teepee-shaped rooms, the Round Barn in Arcadia, Oklahoma, and the U-Drop Inn in Shamrock, Texas, all showcase unique architectural styles that make them must-see stops.

6. Kitschy Souvenirs: Don't forget to pick up some kitschy souvenirs along the way. Route 66-themed gift shops offer a variety of memorabilia, from bumper stickers to postcards, allowing you to take a piece of the quirky charm home with you.

7. Endearing Eccentricities: What makes these attractions special isn't just their oddity but the stories and local legends behind them. The people who maintain these eccentricities often have a deep love for Route 66 and a desire to share its magic with travelers.

As you embark on your Route 66 adventure, make sure to set aside time for these quirky roadside attractions. They're more than just pit stops; they're the spice that adds flavor to your journey and creates lasting memories of the unique and whimsical world of the Mother Road.

Chapter 7: Experiencing Local Culture

One of the most enchanting aspects of a journey along Route 66 is the opportunity to immerse yourself in the vibrant tapestry of local cultures that line the road. As you travel from one state to the next, each with its own unique history, traditions, and flavors, you'll find yourself on a cultural adventure like no other. Route 66 isn't just a highway; it's a corridor of stories, customs, and tastes waiting to be discovered. In this chapter, we'll delve into the diverse and captivating cultures you can experience on your Route 66 odyssey, from the blues of Chicago to the southwestern warmth of Arizona, and every captivating locale in between. Get ready to savor, celebrate, and connect with the soul of America's Main Street.

Art and Music Festivals

Route 66 isn't just a road; it's a cultural journey through the heart of America, and that means an abundance of art and music festivals that showcase the creativity and talent found in every corner of the country. These festivals are a vibrant celebration of both traditional and contemporary arts, as well as a fusion of musical styles that resonate with the diverse communities along the Mother Road. Here are some of the most notable art and music festivals you can experience as you travel Route 66:

1. Chicago Blues Festival, Chicago, Illinois: Start your journey with the soulful strains of blues music at the Chicago Blues Festival. This iconic event, held in Grant Park, pays homage to the genre's roots in the Windy City and features performances by legendary artists and rising stars.

2. International Route 66 Mother Road Festival, Springfield, Illinois: This festival combines classic cars, live music, and a vibrant downtown atmosphere. It's a celebration of all things Route 66, featuring car shows, food vendors, and live entertainment.

3. Birthplace of Route 66 Festival, Springfield, Missouri: Experience the birthplace of Route 66 in Springfield, Missouri, with a festival that includes classic car displays, live music, motorcycle stunt shows, and a parade that honors the road's legacy.

4. Albuquerque International Balloon Fiesta, Albuquerque, New Mexico: While not exclusively an art and music festival, this event combines the artistry of colorful hot air balloons with music and entertainment. It's a dazzling display of creativity against the stunning backdrop of the New Mexico sky.

5. Flagstaff Festival of Science, Flagstaff, Arizona: Explore the wonders of science, art, and culture in Flagstaff. This festival offers lectures, workshops, and art exhibitions that celebrate the intersection of science and creativity.

6. California Route 66 Museum's Car Show and Street Fair, Victorville, California: Immerse yourself in the car culture of Route 66 with this annual event that features classic car displays, live music, and a street fair that captures the spirit of the road.

7. Kingman's Chillin' on Beale Street, Kingman, Arizona: This monthly event celebrates local art, music, and culture in Kingman, Arizona. It's a laid-back gathering where you can enjoy live music and explore the town's creative scene.

8. Joliet Blues Festival, Joliet, Illinois: This festival is a true blues lover's delight. Held in downtown Joliet, it features talented blues musicians from the region, offering a taste of the music that has been intertwined with Route 66 history.

9. Route 66 Summerfest, Albuquerque, New Mexico: Another celebration in Albuquerque, this event combines live music, food, and art in a family-friendly atmosphere. It's a perfect opportunity to soak up the local culture.

10. Tucumcari Rawhide Days, Tucumcari, New Mexico: This lively event in Tucumcari showcases the town's Western heritage with rodeos, live music, and a parade. It's a chance to experience the unique culture of this Route 66 town.

These festivals are more than just entertainment; they're windows into the rich cultural tapestry that lines Route 66. Whether you're a music enthusiast, an art lover, or simply someone looking to soak up the local culture, these events offer a deeper connection to the communities along the Mother Road. As you plan your journey, consider timing your visit to coincide with one of these vibrant celebrations.

Meeting Locals and Immersing in Communities

One of the most rewarding aspects of traveling Route 66 is the opportunity to meet locals and immerse yourself in the unique communities that line the historic highway. Route 66 is not just a road; it's a living, breathing corridor of American culture and community spirit.

Friendly Faces: As you venture along Route 66, you'll encounter the warm hospitality of locals who take pride in their connection to the road. Whether it's a chat with a diner owner about their famous pie recipe or a conversation with a shopkeeper about the history of their town, these interactions add depth to your journey.

Small-Town Charm: Many of the towns along Route 66 exude a timeless charm that's best experienced by mingling with residents. Strolling down Main Streets, attending local events, or simply striking up a conversation at a cafe can provide insights into the heartbeat of these communities.

Festivals and Events: Route 66 communities often host festivals and events that celebrate their unique cultures and traditions. These gatherings offer a chance to participate in local customs, taste regional cuisine, and enjoy the company of both residents and fellow travelers.

Historical Insights: Locals are often the keepers of Route 66's history. They can share stories passed down through generations, recounting the road's heyday and its significance to their communities. Engaging with them provides a richer understanding of the road's evolution.

Supporting Local Businesses: Route 66 is dotted with family-owned businesses that have been serving travelers for decades. By patronizing these establishments, from classic diners to mom-and-pop motels, you contribute to the livelihood of the communities and help preserve the road's heritage.

Hidden Gems: Locals can also reveal hidden gems and off-the-beaten-path attractions that may not be in guidebooks. These unexpected discoveries often become cherished memories of your journey.

Community Involvement: Some Route 66 communities actively engage visitors in local initiatives, such as mural projects or revitalization efforts. Joining in these activities can make you feel like part of the community, leaving a positive impact along your route.

Route 66 isn't just a road trip; it's a cultural expedition. By opening yourself to the people and communities along the way, you'll find that the true treasures of the Mother Road are often the relationships you build and the stories you collect from the locals who call it home.

Cultural Events and Festivals Along Route 66

One of the most captivating aspects of traveling Route 66 is the opportunity to immerse yourself in the rich tapestry of cultural events and festivals that adorn the path of the Mother Road. These celebrations offer a glimpse into the vibrant traditions and diverse heritage of the communities along the way.

- Folk Music and Arts Festivals: Route 66 is a cultural highway, and its festivals reflect this. You'll encounter folk music festivals that showcase the heartwarming melodies and storytelling traditions of the region. Arts festivals bring local creativity to the forefront, with exhibitions and performances that capture the essence of each community.

- Native American Powwows: In states like New Mexico and Arizona, Route 66 intersects with Native American lands. Attending a powwow provides a chance to witness the mesmerizing dances, intricate artwork, and sacred rituals of indigenous cultures. These events foster cultural exchange and appreciation.

- Historical Reenactments: Some communities along Route 66 host historical reenactments that transport you back in time. These living history events offer a window into the past, allowing you to experience the sights and sounds of bygone eras, from pioneer days to the Wild West.

- Culinary Festivals: Food is a universal language, and Route 66 communities celebrate their culinary traditions with gusto. From chili cook-offs in Texas to green chile festivals in New Mexico, you'll have the chance to savor regional flavors and join in the festivities.

- Classic Car Shows: Route 66 has deep ties to the American love affair with automobiles. Classic car shows and rallies are common events along the road, where vintage vehicles take center stage. These gatherings are a testament to the enduring fascination with automotive history.

- Ethnic Celebrations: As you journey westward, you'll encounter communities representing a myriad of ethnic backgrounds. Route 66 plays host to a range of ethnic celebrations, from Oktoberfests in Missouri to Dia de los Muertos festivals in California, allowing you to partake in diverse cultural experiences.

- Balloon Festivals: The southwestern stretch of Route 66 is renowned for its breathtaking hot air balloon festivals. These events fill the skies with a kaleidoscope of colors, creating a surreal backdrop for your journey.

- Route 66 Parades: Some towns along the route hold Route 66-themed parades that celebrate the road's history and its enduring place in American culture. These parades are a joyful display of local pride and creativity.

- Film Festivals: The magic of Route 66 has often been captured on film. Film festivals along the route showcase movies that pay homage to the road, offering cinematic insights into its allure and significance.

- Community Unity: Beyond their cultural and historical significance, these events foster a sense of community and togetherness. As a traveler, you become part of the collective experience, forging connections with both locals and fellow explorers.

These cultural events and festivals are not only an opportunity to celebrate the heritage of Route 66 but also a chance to participate in the traditions and stories of the road. They transform your journey into a vivid tapestry of culture, history, and human connection.

Chapter 8: Road Trip Tips and Safety

Embarking on a journey along Route 66 is a thrilling adventure filled with exploration, history, and countless memories waiting to be made. To ensure your road trip is as enjoyable and safe as possible, it's essential to be well-prepared and informed. Whether you're a seasoned traveler or hitting the open road for the first time, these road trip tips and safety guidelines will help you make the most of your Route 66 experience while keeping you and your fellow travelers secure.

From planning your itinerary to knowing how to handle unexpected situations on the road, this section will provide you with valuable insights and practical advice for a successful Route 66 adventure. So fasten your seatbelt, grab your map or GPS, and get ready to embark on an unforgettable journey down the Mother Road, armed with the knowledge and tools to make it a safe and enjoyable ride.

Safety Precautions

Traveling along Route 66 is a thrilling and nostalgic experience, but like any road trip, it's essential to prioritize safety. The historic highway spans over 2,400 miles, passing through diverse landscapes and communities. To ensure your journey is enjoyable and secure, here are some safety precautions to consider:

1. Vehicle Maintenance: Before hitting the road, thoroughly inspect your vehicle. Check the brakes, tires, lights, and fluid levels. Ensure your spare tire is in good condition, and you have the necessary tools for roadside repairs.

2. Emergency Kit: Prepare an emergency kit that includes essential items like first aid supplies, a flashlight, extra batteries, a basic toolkit, jumper cables, and a reflective vest. It's wise to carry a fire extinguisher and a portable phone charger as well.

3. Route Planning: Plan your route in advance, including overnight stays and rest stops. Make a list of emergency contact numbers, including those for roadside assistance and local authorities. Share your itinerary with someone who can check in on your progress.

4. Weather Awareness: Route 66 traverses various climates, from deserts to mountains. Be aware of local weather conditions and forecasts, especially in regions prone to extreme temperatures, thunderstorms, or snow.

5. Rest Stops: Fatigue can pose a significant risk on long road trips. Schedule regular rest stops to stretch your legs, hydrate, and take short breaks. If you're feeling tired, it's essential to pull over and rest.

6. Defensive Driving: Exercise defensive driving techniques. Stay alert, obey speed limits, and maintain a safe following distance. Be cautious of erratic drivers and wildlife, particularly in rural areas.

7. Seatbelts: Ensure that all passengers in your vehicle wear their seatbelts at all times. Seatbelts are a simple but effective safety measure that can save lives in the event of an accident.

8. Distracted Driving: Avoid distractions while driving, such as texting, using a phone, or fiddling with the radio. Stay focused on the road and designate a passenger as the navigator if needed.

9. Fuel and Provisions: Keep your fuel tank reasonably full, as gas stations may be spaced far apart in some areas. Carry ample drinking water and snacks to stay hydrated and energized.

10. Navigation: Use reliable navigation tools, whether it's a GPS device, smartphone app, or physical maps. Be open to adjusting your route if necessary due to road closures or detours.

11. Crime Awareness: While Route 66 is generally safe, exercise common-sense precautions. Lock your vehicle when it's unattended, and don't leave valuable items in plain sight. Choose well-lit and reputable accommodations for overnight stays.

12. Medical Considerations: If you have specific medical needs or conditions, ensure you have an ample supply of medications and any necessary medical documents. Familiarize yourself with nearby medical facilities along your route.

13. Roadside Assistance: Consider joining a roadside assistance program for added peace of mind. Many organizations offer services like towing, tire changes, and emergency fuel delivery.

By prioritizing safety and preparedness, you can fully enjoy the journey along Route 66 while minimizing risks. Remember that the road's allure lies in its history, culture, and scenic beauty, and taking precautions ensures that you can savor every moment of this iconic adventure.

Car Maintenance on the Road

Maintaining your vehicle while traveling along Route 66 is crucial for a smooth and trouble-free journey. The historic highway presents a variety of road conditions and distances between services, so being proactive about car maintenance can prevent breakdowns and ensure your road trip remains enjoyable. Here are essential car maintenance tips for the road:

1.Pre-Trip Inspection: Before embarking on your Route 66 road trip, it's crucial to perform a thorough pre-trip inspection of your vehicle to ensure a safe and trouble-free journey. Start by checking the engine oil; use the dipstick to verify that it's at the recommended level and appears clean. Inspect the transmission fluid by consulting your owner's manual for the dipstick's location, ensuring it's adequately filled and in good condition. Next, assess the brake fluid by inspecting the reservoir to ensure it's filled correctly and doesn't show signs of contamination. Check the coolant level either in the radiator or reservoir, making sure it's within the recommended range and clean. Don't forget to confirm that your windshield washer fluid reservoir is full for clear visibility.
Moving on to the tires, examine them closely. Check the tire pressure using a gauge and adjust it to the recommended PSI listed in your vehicle's manual. Proper inflation is vital for safety and fuel efficiency. Measure the tread depth with a tread

depth gauge or perform the penny test to ensure it's not too worn; if you can see the top of Lincoln's head on a penny inserted into the tread, it's time to replace the tires. Additionally, inspect the tires for any wear, cuts, bulges, or punctures on both the tread and sidewalls.

Lastly, scrutinize the condition of your vehicle's belts and hoses. Look for signs of wear, cracks, fraying, or any damage on belts like the serpentine belt and hoses like radiator hoses. These components are critical for the proper functioning of your vehicle's systems, and addressing any issues beforehand can prevent potential problems during your road trip.

Completing this comprehensive pre-trip inspection helps ensure your vehicle's reliability, safety, and fuel efficiency on the open road. Addressing any identified issues before your journey gives you peace of mind and minimizes the risk of breakdowns, allowing you to fully enjoy the Route 66 experience. If you're uncertain about any aspect of the inspection, it's advisable to consult a professional mechanic for a thorough assessment.

2. Tire Care: Tire care is of paramount importance when embarking on a Route 66 adventure, considering the varying terrains and conditions you'll encounter. Start by confirming that your tires are correctly inflated according to the manufacturer's recommendations. Proper tire pressure is not only vital for safety but also contributes to fuel efficiency. Along with this, always carry essential tire maintenance tools with you, including a spare tire, jack, lug wrench, and a tire repair kit.

Route 66 spans regions with diverse climates, so it's advisable to periodically check your tire pressure during your journey, particularly when transitioning from extreme heat to cooler temperatures or vice versa. Fluctuations in temperature can affect tire pressure, and maintaining optimal pressure ensures even wear and a smoother ride. Regular inspections of your tires for wear, cuts, or punctures are also essential.

By taking these tire care precautions, you enhance your safety and minimize the risk of unexpected tire-related issues, allowing you to make the most of your Route 66 experience with peace of mind.

3. Fluids and Filters: Maintaining the health of your vehicle's fluids and filters is a fundamental aspect of ensuring a smooth and safe Route 66 journey. Begin by routinely checking and replenishing all vital fluids to keep your engine running optimally. This includes monitoring the engine oil level and quality, the coolant level to prevent overheating, the brake fluid reservoir for safe braking, and the windshield washer fluid for clear visibility during your travels.

In addition to fluid care, consider the condition of your air filters. Regularly inspect and replace the engine air filter as well as the cabin air filter if they become clogged or excessively dirty. A clean engine air filter promotes efficient combustion and engine performance, while a fresh cabin air filter ensures clean air inside the vehicle.

Furthermore, it's wise to carry extra quantities of essential fluids like engine oil and coolant in your vehicle. These provisions can prove invaluable in case of emergencies or when traveling through remote areas with limited access to services. By meticulously tending to your vehicle's fluids and filters, you're taking proactive steps to enhance its reliability and your overall safety during your Route 66 adventure.

4. Battery Health: Battery health is a critical aspect of ensuring your vehicle's reliability on the Route 66 journey. Begin by visually inspecting the battery for any signs of corrosion on the terminals or loose connections. Clean any corrosion with a battery cleaning brush and ensure the terminals are securely fastened to prevent electrical issues. If your vehicle's battery is several years old and exhibits signs of weakness, it's advisable to have it tested by a professional mechanic or an auto parts store. Weak or failing batteries can lead to starting problems, especially in extreme weather conditions.

As an essential precaution, carry jumper cables or a portable jump starter in your vehicle. These tools can be invaluable in case your battery unexpectedly fails, allowing you to jumpstart your vehicle or assist another traveler in need.

By addressing battery health concerns before your Route 66 adventure and equipping yourself with the necessary tools, you'll significantly reduce the risk of being stranded due to battery-related issues, ensuring a more enjoyable and worry-free journey.

5. Brakes and Lights: The condition of your vehicle's brakes and lights is paramount for both safety and legal compliance while traveling along Route 66. Before hitting the road, thoroughly inspect your brakes to ensure they are in good condition. Check the brake pads for sufficient life; worn-out brake pads can compromise your ability to stop safely. If you notice any signs of brake issues, such as squeaking or reduced stopping power, have them examined and serviced by a qualified mechanic. Another vital aspect of vehicle safety is ensuring that all exterior lights are functioning correctly. Test your headlights, taillights, turn signals, and brake lights to confirm that they are working as intended. Promptly replace any burnt-out bulbs to maintain visibility and signal your intentions to other drivers on the road.

By meticulously attending to the condition of your brakes and lights, you enhance your vehicle's safety, reduce the risk of accidents, and ensure compliance with traffic regulations. This proactive approach contributes to a more secure and enjoyable Route 66 journey.

6. Belts and Hoses: The inspection of serpentine belts and hoses is a crucial aspect of vehicle maintenance to safeguard against potential engine issues and overheating during your Route 66 adventure. Carefully examine these components for any visible signs of wear, cracks, or deterioration. Over time, exposure to heat and the elements can cause belts and hoses to weaken, making them susceptible to failure.

To prepare for unexpected situations on the road, consider carrying spare belts and hoses that are compatible with your vehicle's make and model. Having these replacement parts readily available can prove invaluable if you encounter a situation where a belt or hose requires immediate attention. This precautionary measure enhances your vehicle's reliability and ensures you can address unexpected breakdowns swiftly and efficiently. By regularly inspecting and, when necessary, replacing serpentine belts and hoses, as well as carrying spare parts, you minimize the risk of experiencing engine-related issues that could disrupt your Route 66 journey. This proactive approach promotes a more stress-free and enjoyable travel experience.

7. Tools and Emergency Kit: A well-equipped toolkit and an emergency kit are indispensable companions for your Route 66 journey, providing you with the means to address minor vehicle issues and respond to unexpected emergencies. Here's why each of these components is essential:

- 1. Toolkit: A basic toolkit comprising pliers, screwdrivers, wrenches, and a tire pressure gauge enables you to perform minor repairs or adjustments on the road. Whether it's tightening a loose bolt or checking tire pressure, having the right tools at your disposal can help you keep your vehicle in optimal condition and reduce the risk of breakdowns.

- 2. Emergency Kit: An emergency kit contains crucial items to ensure your safety and well-being in unexpected situations. It typically includes a flashlight and spare batteries for visibility during nighttime emergencies, a reflective vest to enhance your visibility to other drivers, first aid supplies to tend to minor injuries, and a fire extinguisher for handling potential vehicle fires.

By equipping your vehicle with these tools and an emergency kit, you empower yourself to handle a range of situations, from minor roadside repairs to providing immediate assistance in the event of an accident or injury. These preparations enhance your safety and peace of mind as you embark on your Route 66 adventure.

8. Check Fluid Levels Regularly: Maintaining your vehicle's fluid levels and paying attention to warning indicators is essential during your Route 66 journey. Here's why this practice is crucial:

Regularly checking your vehicle's fluid levels ensures that critical components like the engine, transmission, and cooling system operate smoothly throughout your journey. By periodically inspecting your engine oil, coolant, and other vital fluids, you reduce the risk of unexpected breakdowns and costly repairs. This proactive approach allows you to identify and address potential issues before they escalate, helping you maintain the reliability of your vehicle.

Monitoring your engine oil level using the dipstick is a straightforward but effective way to ensure your engine remains adequately lubricated. Engine oil is essential for reducing friction and heat within the engine, preventing wear and tear on critical components. If you notice a significant drop in oil level or any warning lights related to low oil pressure on your dashboard, it's crucial to address these issues promptly. Failure to do so could lead to engine damage or failure.

Coolant plays a vital role in regulating your engine's temperature, preventing it from overheating. Regularly checking the coolant reservoir while the engine is cool and ensuring it's filled to the recommended level is essential. Coolant warning lights or sudden temperature spikes should be taken seriously and investigated promptly to avoid potential overheating issues, which can cause severe engine damage.

Other essential fluids, such as brake fluid and transmission fluid, contribute to the proper functioning of your vehicle's braking and transmission systems. Keeping an eye on these fluid levels is essential for safety and performance. Low brake fluid can compromise your braking ability, while insufficient transmission fluid can lead to transmission problems. Additionally, ensuring your windshield washer fluid is topped up guarantees clear visibility while driving, especially during adverse weather conditions.

Your vehicle's dashboard provides valuable information through warning lights and gauges. Pay close attention to these indicators, especially the temperature gauge and any warning lights related to fluid levels or engine performance. These warning signs can alert you to potential issues before they become severe, allowing you to take corrective action early on.

In summary, regular fluid level checks and diligent monitoring of warning indicators are essential practices to maintain the health and reliability of your vehicle during your Route 66 journey. This proactive approach helps ensure a smooth and trouble-free experience on the open road, reducing the risk of unexpected vehicle issues and enhancing your overall safety and enjoyment.

9. Plan for Oil Changes: Planning for oil changes is a critical aspect of vehicle maintenance while traveling on Route 66. Here's why it's essential:
Engine oil is the lifeblood of your vehicle's engine. It lubricates moving parts, reduces friction, and helps dissipate heat. Over time, engine oil degrades and becomes less effective at performing these vital functions. Regular oil changes are necessary to replace old, contaminated oil with fresh, clean oil, ensuring that your engine continues to run smoothly and efficiently.

Route 66 covers significant distances, and the journey can be demanding on your vehicle, especially if you're traveling in extreme weather conditions or over challenging terrain. Neglecting oil changes can lead to engine wear, reduced fuel efficiency, and even engine damage.

Here are a few key reasons to plan for oil changes during your Route 66 adventure:
1. Maintaining Engine Performance: Fresh oil provides better lubrication, which helps your engine operate at its peak performance. This is particularly crucial during a long road trip when you rely on your vehicle to cover substantial distances.

2. Fuel Efficiency: Regular oil changes contribute to better fuel efficiency. With gas prices fluctuating, ensuring your vehicle is running efficiently can help you save money on fuel costs over the course of your journey.

3. Engine Longevity: Consistent oil changes extend the life of your engine. A well-maintained engine is less likely to suffer from costly breakdowns or repairs, ensuring your Route 66 adventure remains enjoyable and trouble-free.

4. Preventing Overheating: Properly lubricated engine components generate less heat, reducing the risk of overheating. This is especially important when traveling through hot and arid regions along the route.

To plan for oil changes:

- Review your vehicle's maintenance schedule: Consult your owner's manual or the manufacturer's recommendations to determine the recommended oil change intervals for your specific make and model.

- Schedule oil changes in advance: Identify service centers along Route 66 where you can have your oil changed as needed. Consider contacting these facilities in advance to ensure they can accommodate your schedule.

- Monitor your vehicle's oil life indicator: Some modern vehicles come equipped with oil life monitoring systems that calculate when an oil change is due based on driving conditions. Pay attention to these indicators and schedule changes accordingly.

- Keep records: Maintain a record of your oil changes, including the date, mileage, and type of oil used. This documentation can be valuable for warranty purposes and helps you track your vehicle's maintenance history.

By proactively planning for oil changes, you'll keep your vehicle running smoothly, reduce the risk of mechanical issues, and ensure that you can fully enjoy the historic Route 66 experience without disruptions.

10. Professional Inspections: Professional inspections conducted by qualified mechanics offer a level of expertise that surpasses routine checks. These experts have extensive training and experience, allowing them to spot potential issues that might elude the untrained eye. This expertise ensures that your vehicle receives a comprehensive examination, addressing both apparent and hidden concerns. Ensuring your vehicle's safety systems are in optimal condition is paramount on a long journey like Route 66. A professional inspection covers crucial safety components such as brakes, steering, suspension, and tires. Mechanics can identify any wear and tear, damage, or irregularities that might compromise your safety on the road. This safety assurance provides peace of mind as you navigate diverse road conditions.

One of the key advantages of professional inspections is their ability to detect potential problems before they escalate. By identifying issues early, mechanics can recommend preventive maintenance measures. Addressing minor concerns promptly can prevent them from evolving into major breakdowns, saving you both time and money in the long run.

Route 66 offers diverse terrain and driving conditions, from city streets to remote highways. To ensure your vehicle's engine operates efficiently, a professional inspection can fine-tune its performance. Mechanics can make necessary adjustments, replace worn-out components, and optimize your vehicle's engine for better fuel efficiency and overall performance.

Not all vehicle owners are well-versed in every aspect of their car's mechanics. Professional inspections cover a comprehensive list of components, including those you might overlook in your routine checks. Mechanics will assess the exhaust system, belts, hoses, and other critical parts that may not be on your radar. This comprehensive approach addresses any unknown issues that could affect your journey. By investing in professional inspections, you significantly reduce the risk of unexpected breakdowns. Experienced mechanics can identify potential vulnerabilities within your engine, transmission, cooling system, and more. Addressing these issues proactively means you're less likely to find yourself stranded on the side of the road, especially in remote areas along Route 66.

Recording each professional inspection and any associated repairs or maintenance provides you with valuable documentation. This record helps you track the condition of your vehicle over time and can assist in warranty claims if needed. Additionally, it aids in future maintenance planning, ensuring your vehicle remains in top shape well beyond your Route 66 journey. To make the most of professional inspections during your Route 66 adventure, consider establishing a relationship with reputable auto repair shops along the route in advance. This preparation will help you access trustworthy service when needed and ensure a smoother and safer road trip experience.

11. Tire rotation: Tire rotation is an important part of your pre-trip vehicle maintenance, especially when embarking on a lengthy journey like a Route 66 adventure. Here's why it matters:

Firstly, tire rotation ensures even wear on your tires. Over time, tires tend to wear down unevenly due to factors like weight distribution, road conditions, and alignment issues. Uneven wear can lead to reduced traction, handling problems, and a shorter tire lifespan. By rotating your tires regularly, you distribute the wear more evenly, extending the life of your tires and enhancing their performance.

Improved fuel efficiency is another benefit of tire rotation. Unevenly worn tires can increase rolling resistance, making your vehicle work harder and use more fuel. When your tires wear evenly, your vehicle can operate more efficiently, which is particularly important on a long road trip like Route 66 where fuel costs can add up.

Safety is paramount during your journey, and properly rotated tires contribute to that. Even tread depth ensures better traction and handling, especially when encountering varying road conditions along Route 66. It reduces the risk of hydroplaning on wet roads, enhances grip on dry surfaces, and provides stability when maneuvering through curves and turns.

Additionally, rotating your tires helps prevent blowouts. Tire blowouts can be dangerous, especially on remote sections of Route 66 where assistance might be limited. By maintaining even tire wear, you reduce the likelihood of sudden tire failures.

Knowing that your tires are in good condition and evenly worn gives you peace of mind during your trip. You can confidently navigate the diverse terrains and long stretches of this historic highway without the worry of tire-related issues.

Before hitting the road, check your vehicle's owner's manual for recommended tire rotation intervals, which typically range from 6,000 to 8,000 miles. Consider scheduling a tire rotation service as part of your pre-trip preparations to ensure a smoother and safer journey along Route 66.

By proactively maintaining your vehicle and being prepared for common road trip issues, you'll not only enhance your safety but also have peace of mind as you cruise along Route 66. Remember that regular maintenance can prevent costly repairs and disruptions, allowing you to fully enjoy the historic journey ahead.

What to Do in Emergencies?

Emergencies can happen even during a well-planned road trip like one along Route 66. Here's what to do in case of emergencies:

1. Stay Calm: In any emergency situation, the first and most crucial step is to stay calm. Panic can make situations worse.

2. Safety First: Ensure your safety and the safety of your passengers. If you can safely move your vehicle out of the road or to the shoulder, do so. Turn on your hazard lights to alert other drivers.

3. Assess the Situation: Evaluate the nature and severity of the emergency. This could be a breakdown, a collision, a medical issue, or getting lost. Understanding the situation is key to determining your next steps.

4. Call for Help: Depending on the emergency, you may need to call 911 for immediate assistance. Be prepared to provide your location, a description of the situation, and any injuries if applicable.

5. Vehicle Breakdowns: If your vehicle breaks down, try to move to a safe location off the road if possible. Use road flares or reflective triangles to increase visibility. If you have roadside assistance, contact them for help.

6. Medical Emergencies: If someone in your vehicle experiences a medical emergency, call 911 immediately. Follow any medical instructions given by the operator while waiting for help.

7. Lost or Stranded: If you get lost or find yourself stranded in an unfamiliar area, use GPS or map apps to determine your location. If you're still unable to find your way, contact a local tow service or a Route 66 association for assistance.

8. Emergency Kit: Having an emergency kit in your vehicle is wise. It should include items like a flashlight, blankets, first aid supplies, water, non-perishable food, a basic tool kit, and a cellphone charger.

9. Stay with Your Vehicle: If your vehicle becomes inoperable and you're unable to get immediate help, it's generally safer to stay with your vehicle rather than venturing out on foot. Your vehicle provides shelter and is easier for rescuers to locate.

10. Communicate: Keep your loved ones informed about your whereabouts and travel plans. Share your itinerary and periodically check in with them. In case of emergencies, they'll know where to find you.

11. Stay Informed: Tune in to local radio stations for traffic updates and emergency information. Many areas along Route 66 have emergency broadcast systems.

12. Travel Insurance: Consider travel insurance that covers trip interruptions, medical emergencies, and roadside assistance. This can provide peace of mind during your journey.

Remember that Route 66 spans diverse terrains, some of which may be remote. Being prepared for emergencies and knowing how to react can make a significant difference in ensuring your safety and the safety of your fellow travelers.

Chapter 9: Sustainability and Responsible Travel

As we embark on journeys along Route 66 and explore the diverse landscapes, cultures, and communities it traverses, it's essential to consider the impact of our travels on the environment and the places we visit. Sustainability and responsible travel are more than just buzzwords; they are guiding principles that help us minimize our footprint, preserve the natural beauty of Route 66, and contribute positively to the lives of the people who call this iconic highway home. In this chapter, we'll delve into the importance of sustainable and responsible travel practices, providing tips and insights to help you be a conscious traveler along the Mother Road.

Eco-Friendly Travel Tips

Traveling responsibly along Route 66 involves adopting eco-friendly practices to minimize your impact on the environment and support the preservation of this historic corridor. Here are some valuable tips to consider:

1. When embarking on your Route 66 journey with sustainability in mind, one of the fundamental principles is to reduce, reuse, and recycle. By adopting these practices, you can significantly lessen your environmental footprint along the historic route. Carrying reusable items like water bottles, shopping bags, and containers is a simple yet impactful way to reduce single-use plastic waste. Having a reusable water bottle on hand not only helps you stay hydrated throughout your travels but also reduces the need for disposable plastic bottles. Similarly, reusable shopping bags and containers can replace the use of plastic bags and disposable food containers, cutting down on the plastic waste generated during your trip.

To further contribute to eco-friendly travel, keep an eye out for recycling bins along Route 66 and in the communities you visit. Properly disposing of recyclables ensures that materials like plastic, glass, and paper can be processed and reused, rather than ending up in landfills. This small act can make a big difference in minimizing the environmental impact of your journey. By integrating the reduce, reuse, and recycle mantra into your Route 66 adventure, you not only help preserve this iconic highway but also set an example for responsible and sustainable travel practices. It's a positive step toward ensuring the beauty and cultural heritage of Route 66 endure for generations to come.

2. Selecting eco-friendly transportation options is a key consideration for travelers aiming to reduce their environmental impact while exploring Route 66. Your choice of vehicle and how you navigate the iconic highway can significantly contribute to sustainability. One of the primary eco-conscious decisions you can make is to opt for a fuel-efficient or electric vehicle for your journey. Modern vehicles with improved fuel efficiency and low emissions help minimize the carbon footprint of your road trip. Electric cars, in particular, produce zero tailpipe emissions and can be charged at various locations along the route, reducing your reliance on fossil fuels.

Carpooling is another sustainable travel practice that can benefit both the environment and your wallet. If you're traveling with companions, consider sharing a vehicle rather than taking separate cars. Carpooling not only reduces the number of vehicles on the road but also lowers overall fuel consumption and emissions.

When exploring cities along Route 66, explore public transportation options such as buses or trains. Many urban areas offer convenient and eco-friendly public transit systems that can help you navigate without the need for a personal vehicle. Using public transportation not only reduces traffic congestion but also cuts down on greenhouse gas emissions.

By consciously choosing eco-friendly transportation options during your Route 66 journey, you actively contribute to preserving the environment and minimizing your carbon footprint. Your actions can inspire others to make environmentally responsible choices while experiencing this historic highway.

3. Driving responsibly and adopting fuel-efficient habits is an essential aspect of eco-friendly travel along Route 66. By making conscious choices behind the wheel, you can reduce your environmental impact while enjoying the journey. One fundamental practice is maintaining a steady speed while driving. Frequent acceleration and braking can lower fuel efficiency. To conserve fuel, try to anticipate traffic conditions and apply gradual, smooth acceleration and braking. This not only saves fuel but also reduces wear and tear on your vehicle. Excessive

idling can contribute to unnecessary fuel consumption and emissions. When parked, turn off your engine rather than letting it idle. Modern vehicles are designed to consume less fuel when restarted than when idling for extended periods.

Regular vehicle maintenance is critical for optimal fuel efficiency. A well-tuned engine operates more efficiently and emits fewer pollutants. Prior to embarking on your Route 66 adventure, ensure that your vehicle has undergone routine maintenance, including oil changes, air filter replacements, and spark plug checks. Properly inflated tires are crucial for improving gas mileage. Under-inflated tires create more rolling resistance, which reduces fuel efficiency. Check your tire pressure regularly, and follow the manufacturer's recommendations for the correct psi (pounds per square inch) for your specific vehicle.

Through this driving practices, you can maximize fuel efficiency, reduce emissions, and minimize your carbon footprint as you journey along Route 66. These small changes in driving behavior can collectively make a significant positive impact on the environment.

4. Choosing eco-friendly accommodations is an impactful way to contribute to sustainable travel along Route 66. By opting for green lodging options, you can reduce your environmental footprint and support businesses committed to eco-conscious practices. When selecting accommodations, look for hotels, motels, or bed-and-breakfasts that have implemented various sustainability measures. Many eco-friendly establishments use energy-efficient lighting, such as LED or CFL bulbs, which consume less electricity and last longer than traditional incandescent bulbs. This not only reduces energy consumption but also minimizes the need for bulb replacements.

Water conservation is another critical aspect of eco-friendly lodging. Seek accommodations that have installed water-saving fixtures like low-flow showerheads and toilets. These fixtures can significantly reduce water usage without compromising your comfort during your stay.

Waste reduction programs are a hallmark of green accommodations. These establishments often emphasize recycling and proper waste disposal. Look for recycling bins in your room or common areas, and follow the provided guidelines for recycling materials like paper, glass, and plastic. Some eco-conscious accommodations go the extra mile by sourcing organic and locally produced products for their amenities, such as toiletries and breakfast items. Supporting local businesses and reducing the carbon footprint associated with transportation are additional benefits of these choices.

Your choices as a traveler can make a meaningful difference in preserving the beauty and culture of this iconic American highway for future generations to explore and enjoy.

5. Conserving water is a vital aspect of responsible travel along Route 66, especially when journeying through arid regions where water resources may be scarce. By adopting water-saving practices during your trip, you can contribute to the sustainability of local communities and help protect the environment.

One of the simplest ways to conserve water is by being mindful of your water usage in accommodations. When staying in hotels, motels, or other lodging options, consider reusing towels and linens to reduce the frequency of laundry, which consumes both water and energy. Many establishments now encourage guests to indicate when they wish to have their towels and linens replaced, allowing you to play an active role in water conservation.

During your showers, strive to keep them shorter in duration. While it's tempting to luxuriate in a long shower, especially after a day of exploring, shorter showers can significantly reduce water consumption. You can also turn off the tap while brushing your teeth or washing your face, preventing unnecessary water wastage.

If you encounter any plumbing issues in your accommodations, such as leaks or running toilets, be sure to report them promptly to the management. Timely repairs can prevent the unnecessary loss of water and ensure that local water resources are used efficiently.

Beyond your accommodations, when you're out and about exploring the sights and attractions of Route 66, practice water-conscious behaviors, such as using refillable water bottles instead of single-use plastic ones. Many communities along the route provide water refill stations, making it convenient to stay hydrated while minimizing plastic waste.

By conserving water during your journey, you not only reduce your environmental impact but also contribute to the well-being of the regions you visit. Responsible water usage helps ensure that water resources remain available for local residents and future travelers along the historic Route 66.

6. When it comes to responsible travel along Route 66, dining sustainably is an important aspect of minimizing your environmental impact and supporting local communities. By making conscious choices when it comes to food, you can contribute to the preservation of the unique culinary heritage along the route and help ensure that it thrives for generations to come.

One of the most effective ways to support local and sustainable dining is by choosing restaurants and eateries that prioritize locally sourced ingredients. Many communities along Route 66 have vibrant food scenes that celebrate regional flavors and ingredients. When dining out, inquire about the origin of the ingredients used in your meal and opt for dishes that feature locally grown or produced items. This not only supports local farmers and food producers but also reduces the carbon footprint associated with transporting food long distances.

Another crucial aspect of sustainable dining is being mindful of food waste. Order thoughtfully, and avoid ordering excessive amounts of food that may go uneaten. If you have leftovers, consider taking them with you or asking for a takeout container to minimize food waste. By reducing food waste, you help conserve resources and reduce the environmental impact of your dining choices.

When dining in communities along Route 66, look for restaurants and cafes that implement sustainable practices. Some establishments use energy-efficient appliances, practice waste reduction through composting or recycling, and conserve water through the use of eco-friendly fixtures. Supporting such businesses encourages others to adopt sustainable practices and reduces the environmental footprint of the dining industry.

Additionally, consider embracing the local culinary specialties of each region you pass through. Each state along Route 66 has its own unique dishes and flavors waiting to be savored. Trying these local specialties not only provides a rich cultural experience but also supports the local food traditions that make Route 66 a culinary journey.

7. As you journey along Route 66 and explore the various parks, natural areas, and scenic landscapes, it's essential to be a responsible traveler and show respect for the environment. By following Leave No Trace principles and adopting environmentally conscious behaviors, you can help preserve the natural beauty and wildlife habitats found along the route. One fundamental principle to uphold is staying on designated trails and paths. Whether you're hiking in a national park, visiting a wildlife refuge, or simply enjoying a roadside stop, sticking to established trails helps protect fragile ecosystems. Straying off the beaten path can trample vegetation, disturb wildlife habitats, and erode the landscape. Respecting these designated routes ensures that future generations can also enjoy the pristine beauty of these areas.

Wildlife encounters are a common part of the Route 66 experience, and it's essential to observe wildlife from a respectful distance. Never feed wild animals, as it can disrupt their natural behaviors and diets. Feeding wildlife can also lead to health problems for the animals and potentially dangerous encounters for humans. Remember that your actions can impact the well-being of these creatures, so always admire them from afar and avoid any actions that could harm or disrupt their lives. When exploring natural areas along Route 66, avoid collecting plants, rocks, or any natural artifacts. Removing these items not only disrupts the ecosystem but can also be illegal in protected areas. It's best to appreciate the beauty of these places without altering them in any way. Leave the natural environment as you found it to ensure its preservation for future generations.

In addition to respecting wildlife and natural areas, consider your impact on the environment as a whole. Minimize your use of single-use plastics and other disposable items, and properly dispose of any waste you generate during your travels. Keep your surroundings clean by picking up after yourself and even picking up any litter you may encounter, leaving the landscape more beautiful than you found it. When you respect wildlife and natural areas and adhering to Leave No Trace principles, you become a responsible traveler who helps protect the delicate ecosystems and pristine landscapes that make Route 66 a remarkable journey through nature. Your actions can contribute to the conservation of these areas, ensuring they remain a source of inspiration and wonder for all who follow in your footsteps.

8. Reducing energy consumption is a key aspect of responsible travel along Route 66. By making mindful choices about energy use, you can lessen your environmental impact and contribute to a more sustainable journey. One of the simplest ways to reduce energy consumption in your accommodations is to turn off lights, appliances, and HVAC (heating, ventilation, and air conditioning) systems when you're not using them. This practice not only conserves energy but also reduces utility costs for lodging providers. Be diligent about switching off lights and electronic devices when leaving your room or during the day when natural light is sufficient.

Utilizing natural lighting and ventilation is another effective strategy. Open curtains and blinds during the day to allow sunlight into your room, reducing the need for artificial lighting. Similarly, if the weather permits, consider opening windows to let fresh air circulate instead of relying solely on air conditioning or heating. Being conscious of these choices can significantly decrease your energy consumption during your stay. In some accommodations, you may find energy-efficient lighting and appliances already in place. Take advantage of these features, and if you have the option, adjust thermostat settings to conserve energy while maintaining your comfort. Many environmentally conscious lodgings have implemented energy-saving measures, such as LED lighting and smart thermostats, to reduce their carbon footprint.

Additionally, consider participating in any energy-saving programs or initiatives offered by your accommodations. Some hotels and motels encourage guests to help conserve energy and water by providing options to reuse towels and linens instead of daily replacements. Embrace these practices as they align with responsible and sustainable travel principles. By reducing energy consumption during your Route 66 journey, you not only reduce your environmental impact but also contribute to the efforts of lodging providers striving to operate sustainably. These small changes collectively make a difference in preserving the environment and ensuring that future travelers can continue to enjoy the beauty of the Route 66 corridor.

9. Limiting plastic use is a crucial aspect of responsible travel along Route 66, as it helps reduce plastic pollution and its harmful impact on the environment. By making conscious choices to minimize single-use plastics, you can contribute to a cleaner and more sustainable journey. One of the simplest ways to limit plastic use is by saying no to single-use plastic straws, utensils, and containers. When dining at restaurants and eateries along the route, inform your server that you don't need a plastic straw with your beverage. Many establishments are increasingly responsive to these requests and are transitioning to paper or reusable alternatives.

To further reduce plastic waste, consider carrying a reusable straw and utensil set with you during your travels. These compact and lightweight tools are convenient to have on hand, whether you're dining in or grabbing takeout. By using your reusable utensils instead of plastic ones provided by restaurants, you help decrease the demand for single-use plastics. In addition to straws and utensils, be mindful of other single-use plastic items such as plastic bags and water bottles. Carry a reusable shopping bag to use when purchasing souvenirs or groceries along the route. Opt for a reusable water bottle and refill it at water stations or fountains to avoid buying bottled water, which often comes in single-use plastic containers.

Participating in the "Refuse, Reduce, Reuse, Recycle" mantra when it comes to plastics can have a positive impact not only on the Route 66 environment but also on the broader issue of plastic pollution worldwide. By reducing your reliance on single-use plastics and encouraging responsible consumption, you help protect the natural beauty of the Route 66 corridor for future generations to enjoy.
By incorporating these practices into your journey, you become a responsible traveler who actively contributes to reducing plastic waste and promoting a more sustainable approach to experiencing the iconic Route 66.

10. Supporting responsible tourism is a key element of traveling along Route 66 in a sustainable and ethical manner. By making conscious choices and selecting tour

operators and activities that prioritize sustainability and community involvement, you can contribute positively to the regions you visit and help protect the cultural and natural heritage of the Route 66 corridor. One essential aspect of responsible tourism is choosing tour operators and activities that align with sustainable practices. Research and opt for tour companies that are committed to minimizing their environmental impact. Look for operators that use fuel-efficient or electric vehicles, practice waste reduction, and contribute to local conservation efforts. Supporting these operators ensures that your tourist dollars contribute to the preservation of the natural beauty along Route 66.

When engaging in tours and activities, take the opportunity to learn about the local cultures and traditions of the communities you visit. Show respect for the cultural heritage of the region, and be mindful of local customs and etiquette. Engaging respectfully with local communities helps create positive interactions and fosters a sense of mutual appreciation. Consider participating in tours or activities that support local artisans and businesses. Purchasing locally made crafts, artwork, or products can have a positive economic impact on the communities along Route 66. Additionally, buying from local markets and eateries often means you're enjoying authentic, regionally sourced products.

Respect for the environment is another crucial aspect of responsible tourism. When exploring parks and natural areas along Route 66, adhere to Leave No Trace principles. Stay on designated trails, avoid disturbing wildlife, and do not pick plants or remove rocks. Leave the natural beauty of these areas intact for future generations to appreciate.
Furthermore, support responsible tourism by being a considerate and mindful traveler. Minimize waste by practicing proper waste disposal and recycling. Conserve water and energy in your accommodations by turning off lights and appliances when not in use.
By actively supporting responsible tourism, you not only enrich your Route 66 experience but also contribute to the well-being of the communities and environments you encounter along the way. Your responsible choices can help preserve the Route 66 corridor for future generations to enjoy, ensuring that this iconic road remains a symbol of both adventure and sustainability.

11. Minimizing air travel is a sustainable choice when exploring Route 66. While this iconic road trip is often associated with driving, there are alternative, eco-friendly ways to experience the route that can significantly reduce your carbon footprint. One option is to consider cycling along sections of Route 66. Biking allows you to slow down and immerse yourself in the landscapes, cultures, and communities along the route while minimizing your environmental impact. There are dedicated bike trails and cycling-friendly roads along portions of the route, making it accessible for cyclists of various skill levels. Be sure to pack your camping gear or plan accommodations in bike-friendly towns along the way to support your cycling adventure.

Another eco-conscious approach is to explore Route 66 on foot, engaging in long-distance walking or hiking. This method provides a unique, up-close perspective of the terrain and the places you encounter. However, keep in mind that this option requires thorough preparation, including route planning, suitable footwear, and consideration of camping or lodging options along the way. By choosing these alternative modes of travel, you not only reduce your carbon emissions but also gain a deeper connection to the landscapes and communities that Route 66 traverses. Cycling or walking allows you to savor the journey at a slower pace, appreciate the natural beauty, and engage more intimately with the local cultures, all while treading lightly on the environment. It's a sustainable and enriching way to experience the iconic route while minimizing your ecological footprint.

12. "Leave It as You Found It" is a fundamental principle for responsible and sustainable travel along Route 66. This practice is essential to preserve the historic sites, natural landscapes, and cultural heritage that make the route so special. When exploring Route 66, it's crucial to carry any trash or waste with you until you reach designated disposal areas. Dispose of garbage, recyclables, and hazardous materials appropriately, following local guidelines and using recycling bins or trash receptacles. Littering not only detracts from the beauty of the road but also harms the environment and wildlife.

Moreover, when visiting historic sites, landmarks, or natural areas, be respectful and avoid leaving any markings or graffiti. Many of these locations hold significant historical and cultural value, and preserving them for future generations is a shared responsibility. Taking photos and memories with you is a great way to commemorate your journey without causing harm to these iconic places.

If you adhere to the "Leave It as You Found It" principle, you contribute to the sustainability and long-term preservation of Route 66. Your actions can help ensure that this historic highway remains a treasure for travelers and communities alike, now and in the future.

Supporting Local Communities

Supporting local communities along Route 66 is not only a responsible travel practice but also a meaningful way to connect with the people and culture of this iconic road. Here are some key aspects to consider:

- Shop Local: When you visit towns and cities along Route 66, explore local shops, markets, and boutiques. Purchasing handmade crafts, artwork, and souvenirs directly from local artisans and businesses contributes to the local economy and allows you to take home unique and authentic mementos of your journey.

- Dine Locally: Seek out local restaurants, cafes, and eateries that showcase regional cuisine and flavors. By dining at these establishments, you not only savor the true essence of the area but also support local chefs, farmers, and food producers.

- Stay in Independent Lodgings: Choose accommodations that are locally owned, such as boutique hotels, bed and breakfasts, or family-run motels. Staying at these establishments often provides a more personalized and culturally immersive experience, and your patronage directly benefits the local community.

- Engage with Residents: Strike up conversations with local residents, whether it's at a diner, a museum, or a community event. Locals often have valuable insights, stories, and recommendations that can enhance your Route 66 experience. Respect their perspectives and show genuine interest in their community.

- Participate in Local Events: Check the local event calendar for festivals, parades, and cultural events happening along Route 66. Attending these gatherings not only exposes you to the rich tapestry of local traditions but also contributes to the community's vibrancy.

- Respect Local Culture: Be mindful of cultural norms and practices in the areas you visit. Show respect for local customs, traditions, and historical sites. Responsible travelers honor the heritage and identity of the communities they encounter.

- Volunteer and Give Back: Consider giving back to the communities you visit by participating in volunteer programs or supporting local charities and nonprofits. Even a small contribution or a few hours of your time can make a positive impact.

By supporting local communities along Route 66, you become an active participant in the journey, forging connections with the people and places that make this historic highway so special. Your engagement helps sustain the unique character and vitality of each town and contributes to the enduring legacy of Route 66.

Reducing Environmental Impact

Reducing your environmental impact while traveling along Route 66 is a responsible and sustainable choice. Here are some eco-friendly practices to consider:

- Choose Fuel-Efficient Transportation: Opt for a fuel-efficient or electric vehicle for your journey. If possible, carpool with others to reduce emissions and fuel consumption. Alternatively, explore cities along Route 66 using public transportation, walking, or cycling.

- Minimize Plastic Use: Say no to single-use plastic straws, utensils, and containers. Instead, carry a reusable straw and utensil set for convenience. Use a refillable water bottle to reduce plastic waste and consider using a reusable shopping bag for souvenirs and groceries.

- Conserve Water: Be mindful of water usage, especially in arid regions along Route 66. Take shorter showers, reuse towels, and promptly report any leaks in your accommodations. Every drop saved contributes to water conservation efforts.

- Reduce Energy Consumption: Turn off lights, appliances, and HVAC systems when not in use in your accommodations. Take advantage of natural lighting and ventilation to reduce electricity consumption. Using energy-efficient lighting also helps minimize your carbon footprint.

- Support Green Accommodations: Seek lodging options that have implemented eco-friendly practices. Look for accommodations with energy-efficient lighting, water-saving fixtures, and waste reduction programs. By choosing green lodgings, you support environmentally responsible businesses.

- Support Local and Sustainable Dining: Choose restaurants and eateries that prioritize locally sourced and sustainable ingredients. By dining responsibly, you help reduce the carbon footprint associated with food transportation and support local farmers and food producers.

- Leave No Trace: When exploring natural areas and parks along Route 66, follow Leave No Trace principles. Stay on designated trails, avoid disturbing wildlife, and do not pick plants or remove rocks. Leave these areas as you found them, ensuring their preservation for future generations.

- Minimize Air Travel: Consider exploring sections of Route 66 by other means, such as cycling or walking, to reduce the carbon emissions associated with air travel. Additionally, plan your trip efficiently to reduce the need for long flights.

- Participate in Environmental Initiatives: Look for opportunities to join environmental initiatives or volunteer programs during your journey. Many communities along Route 66 engage in conservation efforts, and your participation can make a positive impact.

- Educate Yourself: Learn about the environmental challenges faced by the regions you visit along Route 66. Understanding the local context and issues allows you to make informed choices that align with responsible travel practices.

By adopting these eco-friendly practices, you can enjoy your Route 66 adventure while minimizing your environmental impact and contributing to the preservation of the road's natural beauty and cultural heritage. Responsible travel ensures that future generations can continue to experience the magic of Route 66.

Chapter 10: Beyond Route 66

Beyond Route 66, there exists a world of exploration and discovery, where new adventures await those who are eager to embark on journeys beyond the iconic highway. While Route 66 itself is a historic and captivating route, it serves as a gateway to a myriad of destinations, landscapes, and experiences.

In this chapter, we'll venture off the beaten path and explore the diverse opportunities that lie beyond Route 66's famous stretches of road. Whether you're seeking natural wonders, cultural encounters, or urban escapades, the areas surrounding Route 66 are brimming with possibilities for further exploration. Join us as we step off the highway and into the broader tapestry of American travel.

Side Trips and Extensions

While Route 66 itself offers a wealth of experiences, consider incorporating side trips and extensions into your journey to explore nearby attractions and regions. Here are some enticing options:

1. Grand Canyon National Park (Detour): When your Route 66 journey takes you near the Grand Canyon, it's a detour that's absolutely worth it. This iconic national park is renowned for its awe-inspiring beauty and breathtaking vistas. As you venture from Route 66, you'll find yourself immersed in a natural wonder that's unparalleled in its grandeur. The Grand Canyon offers a myriad of experiences to suit all interests. You can stand at the edge of the South Rim and gaze out over the vast chasm, marveling at the layers of colorful rock that tell the Earth's geological history. For the more adventurous, hiking trails like the Bright Angel Trail and South Kaibab Trail provide opportunities to descend into the canyon, revealing a unique perspective and offering memorable encounters with its rugged terrain.

If you're looking for an even more exhilarating adventure, consider a helicopter tour. Soaring above the canyon allows you to appreciate its immense scale and beauty from a bird's-eye view. It's a thrilling way to capture the grandeur of this natural wonder in all its glory.

Whether you're a nature enthusiast, a photographer, or simply someone who appreciates the splendors of the great outdoors, the Grand Canyon is a detour that will leave you with unforgettable memories. It's a testament to the diverse and remarkable landscapes that can be discovered just a short distance from Route 66.

2. Joshua Tree National Park (Detour): Heading west from Route 66, you'll find yourself in the surreal and captivating landscapes of Joshua Tree National Park. This detour offers a stark contrast to the historic road's typical scenery, as you enter a realm of unique rock formations, stark deserts, and a sense of otherworldly beauty. Joshua Tree National Park is renowned for its distinctive namesake trees, the Joshua trees, which are unlike any other plant species you'll encounter on your journey along Route 66. These spiky, otherworldly trees create a landscape that feels like something out of a science fiction novel.

One of the primary draws of the park is its excellent hiking opportunities. Trails wind through the rocky terrain, leading you to hidden oases, rugged peaks, and panoramic viewpoints. For the adventurous, Joshua Tree is a rock climber's paradise, with challenging formations that attract climbers from around the world. Stargazing in Joshua Tree is also exceptional. With minimal light pollution, the night skies are adorned with a blanket of stars. Consider camping overnight to witness the celestial beauty of the Milky Way and countless constellations. This detour is a chance to step into a uniquely American desert landscape, where the interplay of rock, sky, and Joshua trees creates an almost surreal environment. It's a journey within a journey that showcases the incredible diversity of natural wonders you can explore alongside Route 66.

3. The Hollywood Sign and Walk of Fame (Detour): Heading south from the final stretch of Route 66, you'll find yourself in the heart of Los Angeles, a city synonymous with the entertainment industry. This detour offers you a chance to immerse yourself in the glitz and glamour of Hollywood. The iconic Hollywood Sign stands tall on the hills overlooking the city. It's a symbol of dreams, ambition, and the allure of the silver screen. While you can't get too close to the sign itself, various viewpoints around the city provide excellent photo opportunities.

Another must-visit attraction is the Hollywood Walk of Fame, where over 2,600 brass stars embedded in the sidewalks honor notable celebrities. You can stroll down Hollywood Boulevard, marveling at the names of actors, musicians, directors, and other entertainment luminaries who've left their mark on the entertainment world. Hollywood offers a range of entertainment experiences. You can catch a live performance at one of the historic theaters, attend a movie premiere, or even take a guided tour of celebrity homes. And, of course, there are countless dining options where you might spot a celebrity or two.

Los Angeles is a city with a rich cinematic history, and it's a detour that allows you to dive into the magic of the movies and perhaps catch a glimpse of the stars, both on the sidewalks and in the sky. While it's a departure from Route 66's historic charm, it's a detour that encapsulates a different aspect of American culture - the world of entertainment.

4. Santa Fe, New Mexico (Detour): A detour to Santa Fe is an immersion into the rich cultural tapestry of New Mexico. Known for its distinctive adobe architecture, art galleries, and vibrant food scene, Santa Fe offers a unique blend of history and creativity. Start your exploration in the heart of the city at the historic Santa Fe Plaza. This centuries-old gathering place is surrounded by adobe buildings and is home to events, markets, and festivals throughout the year. It's an excellent spot to soak in the city's atmosphere.

Art enthusiasts will find Santa Fe to be a haven. The city boasts numerous art galleries and studios showcasing everything from traditional Native American art to contemporary works. The Georgia O'Keeffe Museum pays homage to one of America's most renowned artists, while Canyon Road is an art lover's paradise, with galleries lining this picturesque street.

Santa Fe's culinary scene is equally enticing. The city's cuisine is a fusion of Native American, Spanish, and Mexican influences. Be sure to savor dishes like green chile stew and indulge in the city's famous sopapillas.

For history buffs, Santa Fe offers a glimpse into its past through museums like the New Mexico History Museum and the Palace of the Governors, the oldest continuously used public building in the United States.

The city's Pueblo-style architecture and its commitment to preserving its cultural heritage make it a distinctive and memorable detour from Route 66. Whether you're an art enthusiast, a history buff, or a foodie, Santa Fe has something to offer every traveler seeking a deeper connection with the cultural diversity of the American Southwest.

5. Las Vegas, Nevada (Detour): A detour to Las Vegas promises a vibrant, thrilling, and entirely different experience from the historic charm of Route 66. Known as the "Entertainment Capital of the World," Las Vegas offers an electrifying contrast to the classic American road trip. Las Vegas is synonymous with world-famous casinos and resorts that line the iconic Las Vegas Strip. Whether you're a seasoned gambler or just curious, the casinos provide an atmosphere of opulence, excitement, and non-stop entertainment. Test your luck at the blackjack table, spin the roulette wheel, or try your hand at the slot machines.
Beyond the casinos, Las Vegas is renowned for its world-class entertainment. Catch a spectacular live show featuring renowned artists, acrobats, magicians, and more. The city's theaters and performance venues host an array of productions that cater to every taste.

If you seek a break from the glitz and glamour, the surrounding natural wonders provide a striking contrast. A visit to Red Rock Canyon National Conservation Area is a must for outdoor enthusiasts. This desert oasis offers hiking trails, rock climbing, and opportunities for photography amid stunning red rock formations. Las Vegas also serves as a gateway to the nearby Hoover Dam, a marvel of engineering that spans the Colorado River. Take a tour to learn about its history and significance. The city's dining scene is a world unto itself, featuring celebrity chef-driven restaurants, international cuisines, and all-you-can-eat buffets. From gourmet dining to late-night snacks, Las Vegas caters to every palate.
Las Vegas is a city that never sleeps, and while it may be a departure from the historical Route 66 experience, it offers a dazzling detour filled with entertainment, excitement, and indulgence. Whether you're drawn to the casinos, the shows, or the natural wonders, Las Vegas is a detour you won't soon forget.

6. Sedona, Arizona (Detour): Embarking on a detour to Sedona promises a breathtaking encounter with nature's artistry and a tranquil desert escape. Sedona is renowned for its mesmerizing red rock formations, which stand like ancient sentinels against the Arizona sky. These striking formations have been

sculpted over millions of years by wind and water, creating a landscape that seems otherworldly. As you approach this desert town, the towering red buttes and mesas serve as an awe-inspiring prelude to your Sedona adventure.

Hiking enthusiasts will find a paradise of trails to explore. Some of the most famous include Cathedral Rock, Bell Rock, and Devil's Bridge. These hikes offer various levels of difficulty and the opportunity to witness Sedona's iconic red rock up close. The rewards are plentiful, with sweeping vistas, natural arches, and the serenity of the desert.

For a different perspective, consider taking a guided jeep tour. Knowledgeable guides will navigate you through rugged terrain, revealing the geological wonders and sharing stories of Sedona's history and spirituality. Sunset jeep tours offer an enchanting view as the rocks light up with fiery hues. The town of Sedona itself is a haven for art enthusiasts. Galleries showcasing a wide range of artistic styles can be found throughout the area. The arts scene here is a reflection of the stunning landscapes that have inspired artists for generations. As you explore Sedona, you'll also encounter vortex sites, which are believed to emit powerful energy. Many visitors come seeking spiritual experiences and self-discovery at these locations. To complete your Sedona experience, indulge in the town's upscale dining options, boutique shopping, and luxurious spas. Sedona's culinary scene showcases southwestern flavors with a gourmet twist.

Sedona's unique blend of natural wonder, artistic spirit, and spiritual energy makes it an inviting detour from Route 66. Whether you're drawn to hiking, jeep tours, art, or simply the tranquility of the desert, Sedona offers a captivating escape into Arizona's red rock paradise.

7. Carlsbad Caverns National Park (Detour): Venture to the depths of southeastern New Mexico to discover the enchanting underground realm of Carlsbad Caverns. Carved over eons by the relentless work of water and time, Carlsbad Caverns is a testament to the mesmerizing beauty of subterranean landscapes. This national park boasts one of the most extensive cave systems in the world, and it's a place where you can step into the heart of the Earth's geological wonders.

As you descend into the caverns, you'll be met with a surreal world of intricate formations. Stalactites hang like chandeliers, while stalagmites rise from the ground in surreal, cathedral-like formations. The Big Room, one of the largest cave chambers on the planet, will leave you in awe as you explore its expansive depths. One of the park's most iconic experiences is witnessing the nightly bat flight. Thousands of Mexican free-tailed bats pour out of the cavern entrance in search of their evening meal. This natural spectacle is a reminder of the interconnectedness of the natural world.

Exploring Carlsbad Caverns can be as adventurous or as leisurely as you desire. Guided tours are available, ranging from easy walks suitable for all ages to more challenging explorations for the intrepid caver. Above ground, the desert landscape of the park offers hiking trails and opportunities for wildlife viewing. Keep an eye out for mule deer, roadrunners, and desert birds that call this rugged terrain home. Carlsbad Caverns National Park is a detour that will transport you to a world rarely seen by the surface-dwelling traveler. Its subterranean splendor, combined with the stark beauty of the Chihuahuan Desert, creates an unforgettable journey into the Earth's depths.

8. Albuquerque International Balloon Fiesta (Seasonal): If your Route 66 adventure falls within the right time frame, consider adding a dash of color and wonder to your trip with the Albuquerque International Balloon Fiesta.
Held annually in Albuquerque, New Mexico, this spectacular event is a visual feast for the senses. Imagine the sky filled with hundreds of hot air balloons, each in vibrant hues and imaginative shapes. From classic teardrop balloons to whimsical character designs, you'll witness a stunning array of floating artwork.

The fiesta typically spans several days, offering ample opportunities to join in the festivities. One of the most captivating moments is the Mass Ascension, where hundreds of balloons take to the sky in synchronized fashion. As the sun rises over the Sandia Mountains, the balloons ascend, creating a breathtaking vista of colors against the morning light.
Beyond the Mass Ascension, you can explore the grounds and get up close to the balloons and their crews. It's a chance to learn about the art and science of hot air ballooning and even chat with the pilots.

If you're feeling adventurous, consider taking a hot air balloon ride yourself. Drifting above the Rio Grande Valley and the city of Albuquerque is a serene and magical experience that you won't soon forget.

The Albuquerque International Balloon Fiesta is not only a visual spectacle but also a celebration of New Mexico's culture. You'll find delicious local cuisine, live music, and cultural performances throughout the event.
Keep in mind that the fiesta usually takes place in early October, so plan your Route 66 journey accordingly to catch this vibrant and uplifting experience. The sight of colorful balloons against the New Mexico sky will leave you with memories that soar high above the open road.

9. Zion National Park (Detour): If you're eager to explore nature's grandeur beyond Route 66, consider a detour to the majestic Zion National Park in southwestern Utah.
Zion is a land of towering red rock formations, deep canyons, and serene rivers. It's a paradise for outdoor enthusiasts, hikers, and photographers. The park offers a diverse range of activities, and you can customize your visit to match your interests and available time.
One of the most renowned experiences at Zion is hiking the Narrows. This trail leads you into the heart of the Virgin River Narrows, where the canyon walls soar thousands of feet above you, and the river becomes your path. Hike through water, surrounded by breathtaking sandstone cliffs that seem to touch the sky. It's an adventure that will make you feel small amidst nature's grandeur.

For those looking for a less challenging hike, the Emerald Pools trail system offers a rewarding journey through lush landscapes leading to cascading waterfalls. The Observation Point Trail and the Angels Landing Trail are more strenuous but provide sweeping vistas of the park. If you prefer a more relaxed visit, take the Zion Canyon Scenic Drive, which offers breathtaking views from the comfort of your vehicle. There are also shuttle services available within the park to reduce traffic and ease transportation. While Zion National Park can be visited year-round, spring and fall tend to be the most pleasant times due to milder temperatures. If you plan to hike, wear appropriate footwear and be prepared for changing weather conditions.

Detouring to Zion National Park from Route 66 is an opportunity to immerse yourself in the striking natural beauty of the American Southwest. Whether you're an avid hiker or simply seek to admire awe-inspiring landscapes, Zion is a detour well worth taking on your journey.

These side trips and extensions allow you to tailor your Route 66 adventure to your interests, whether you're drawn to natural wonders, cultural experiences, or urban exploration. Take the opportunity to go beyond the highway and discover the diverse treasures that surround Route 66.

Connecting to Other Scenic Byways

Route 66, often referred to as the "Main Street of America," isn't the only iconic scenic byway in the United States. When planning your Route 66 adventure, consider extending your journey by connecting to other scenic byways nearby. Here are some notable options:

1. The Great River Road: The Great River Road presents a fantastic opportunity to extend your Route 66 adventure by following the winding path of the Mississippi River. Spanning ten states, this iconic scenic byway offers a diverse array of experiences. As you journey along the riverbanks, you'll be treated to breathtaking vistas of the mighty Mississippi, showcasing its powerful currents and serene backwaters. One of the defining features of the Great River Road is its rich historical heritage. You can explore numerous historic sites, museums, and landmarks that tell the story of the river's importance in shaping the nation's history. From Civil War battlefields to Native American heritage sites, the byway immerses you in a rich tapestry of American history.

Charming river towns dot the route, each with its own unique character. These towns offer a warm welcome to travelers, with friendly locals, riverside parks, and delightful cafes and shops. Exploring these communities allows you to connect with the culture and traditions of the region. The Great River Road is also a haven for nature enthusiasts. It traverses through various ecosystems, providing opportunities for birdwatching, hiking, and water-based activities like boating and fishing. The byway's changing landscapes make it an ideal route for those who appreciate the beauty of the great outdoors.

As you journey along the Great River Road, you'll find yourself crossing state lines and encountering diverse regional cuisines. From Southern comfort food to Midwestern specialties, the culinary experiences along this route are as diverse as the landscapes. Be sure to savor regional delicacies and local flavors in the charming eateries you encounter. Connecting to the Great River Road after your Route 66 expedition allows you to embark on a new adventure, exploring America's heartland from a different perspective. Whether you're drawn to history, natural beauty, or simply the allure of the Mississippi River, this scenic byway offers a rewarding continuation of your road trip.

2. **Blue Ridge Parkway:** Extending your road trip adventure beyond Route 66 is an enticing option, and one remarkable way to do so is by connecting to the **Blue Ridge Parkway**. This iconic byway, often referred to as "America's Favorite Drive," takes you on a scenic journey through the Appalachian Highlands, offering a striking contrast to the landscapes you've encountered along Route 66.
The Blue Ridge Parkway is celebrated for its captivating mountain vistas. As you wind your way along its serpentine roads, you'll be treated to breathtaking panoramic views of the Appalachian Mountains. Towering peaks, rolling hills, and deep valleys create a landscape that's a paradise for nature enthusiasts and photographers alike.

One of the notable features of this byway is its extensive network of hiking trails. These trails range from easy strolls to challenging backcountry hikes, allowing you to explore the pristine beauty of the Appalachian wilderness. Whether you're interested in a leisurely walk to a scenic overlook or an immersive trek through dense forests, the Blue Ridge Parkway has a trail for you.
If your road trip coincides with the fall season, you're in for a treat. The Blue Ridge Parkway is renowned for its vibrant fall foliage, with the leaves of hardwood trees turning brilliant shades of red, orange, and gold. Timing your journey during this period will reward you with a symphony of autumn colors that's nothing short of awe-inspiring. The small towns and communities along the Blue Ridge Parkway

provide a warm and inviting atmosphere. You'll find charming mountain towns where you can explore local crafts, savor regional cuisine, and interact with friendly locals. These towns offer a glimpse into the unique Appalachian culture.

Connecting to the Blue Ridge Parkway after your Route 66 expedition is like embarking on a completely different road trip. It's an opportunity to immerse yourself in the beauty of the Appalachian Mountains, enjoy outdoor adventures, and experience the vibrant culture of the region. Whether you're drawn to stunning vistas, hiking trails, or the magic of fall foliage, this scenic byway offers a captivating extension to your journey.

3. Pacific Coast Highway (California State Route 1): Extending your Route 66 adventure to the West Coast offers the perfect opportunity to connect with another legendary American road, the **Pacific Coast Highway**, also known as **California State Route 1**. This scenic highway, meandering along the breathtaking California coastline, provides a fitting continuation of your road trip. As you head southward from the endpoint of Route 66 in Santa Monica, California, you'll be welcomed by the shimmering Pacific Ocean on one side and the rugged landscapes of California's coastline on the other. The Pacific Coast Highway is renowned for its dramatic vistas, offering panoramic views of the ocean, cliffs, and coves that define California's shoreline.

One of the standout highlights of this route is **Big Sur**, a region celebrated for its natural beauty and awe-inspiring landscapes. Here, you can explore state parks, hike through ancient redwood forests, and gaze out over the iconic Bixby Creek Bridge. Big Sur also offers serene beaches, making it a fantastic place to unwind and soak in the coastal ambiance. The Pacific Coast Highway also grants access to numerous charming coastal towns and cities, each with its own unique character. You can visit **Monterey** to explore the famous **Monterey Bay Aquarium**, indulge in fresh seafood, or take a scenic drive along **17-Mile Drive**. Further south, you'll find **Carmel-by-the-Sea**, known for its artistic community and picturesque cottages.

Continuing your journey, you'll reach **Pebble Beach**, home to world-renowned golf courses and iconic landscapes. **Pacific Grove** beckons with its lovely Victorian homes and monarch butterfly sanctuary. And as you venture even further south, the vibrant city of **Santa Barbara** awaits, with its Spanish colonial architecture, inviting beaches, and diverse cultural attractions.

The Pacific Coast Highway is an ideal route for travelers who appreciate stunning coastal views, outdoor adventures, and the serene beauty of the California shoreline. Whether you're captivated by the allure of Big Sur, the charm of coastal towns, or the allure of the Pacific Ocean, this extension of your Route 66 journey promises to be an unforgettable experience.

4. U.S. Route 50, often referred to as the Loneliest Road in America, beckons adventurers seeking a unique journey. This extensive highway, stretching from the shores of Maryland to the golden state of California, promises an experience quite unlike any other. The Loneliest Road in America is aptly named, as it offers travelers a profound sense of solitude that's rare in today's bustling world.

One of the defining features of this road is the vast expanse of wide-open spaces it traverses. As you drive along U.S. Route 50, you'll be met with seemingly endless stretches of untouched landscapes, where the horizon stretches out as far as the eye can see. The sheer emptiness of these surroundings can be both awe-inspiring and humbling, inviting introspection and a deep connection with nature.

In addition to the solitude and natural beauty, U.S. Route 50 is also home to a myriad of quirky roadside attractions. Along this lonely stretch of highway, you'll encounter peculiar and charming stops that break the monotony of the road. These quirky attractions add an element of surprise to your journey, making it an adventure filled with unexpected discoveries. In essence, the Loneliest Road in America, U.S. Route 50, beckons those who yearn for an unconventional adventure. It's a road that allows you to escape the hustle and bustle of city life, offering solitude amidst breathtaking landscapes while sprinkling in moments of whimsy and wonder through its eccentric roadside attractions. This highway is an invitation to explore the less-traveled path and discover the beauty of America's untamed heartland.

5. Highway 101 (Oregon Coast): Highway 101 along the Oregon Coast is an essential addition to your Pacific Northwest exploration. This scenic byway offers travelers a taste of rugged coastal beauty, with breathtaking scenery at every turn. Along the route, you'll encounter charming beach towns that beckon you to explore their unique character and culture. One of the standout features of Highway 101 is the opportunity for beachcombing, allowing you to discover treasures brought in by the Pacific Ocean. The coastline is also known for its whale-watching spots, where you can catch glimpses of these majestic creatures as they migrate along the coast. So, when venturing through the Pacific Northwest, be sure to include Highway 101 on your itinerary. It promises a journey filled with stunning coastal landscapes, delightful seaside communities, and exciting opportunities to connect with nature.

6. Embarking on the Natchez Trace Parkway in the southern United States is an immersive journey that takes you through a tapestry of history and natural wonder. This scenic route traces the footsteps of an ancient Native American trail, adding layers of cultural significance to your adventure.

As you navigate along the Natchez Trace Parkway, you'll encounter historical markers that offer glimpses into the past, revealing stories of the people and events that shaped this region. The surrounding landscape features lush forests, providing a serene backdrop for your exploration.

This byway beckons history enthusiasts, nature lovers, and anyone seeking a tranquil escape into the heart of the southern United States. It's a route where the past and present seamlessly merge, offering a rich and captivating journey for travelers.

7. Extend your adventure by seamlessly connecting to the San Juan Skyway in the picturesque state of Colorado. This remarkable byway guides you through the breathtaking San Juan Mountains, a region renowned for its awe-inspiring alpine scenery. Travelers along the San Juan Skyway are treated to a visual feast of towering peaks, lush forests, and pristine lakes, making it an ideal route for nature enthusiasts and outdoor adventurers. The surrounding area provides ample

opportunities for hiking, biking, and exploring the great outdoors, allowing you to fully immerse yourself in the splendor of the Rocky Mountains.

Incorporating the San Juan Skyway into your journey promises an unforgettable experience, where the majesty of the natural world takes center stage. Whether you're captivated by mountain landscapes or yearning for thrilling outdoor activities, this byway offers an exceptional opportunity to connect with Colorado's alpine beauty.

8. National Scenic Byway 12 (Utah): Embarking on a journey along the National Scenic Byway 12 in Utah offers travelers an incredible detour through the mesmerizing landscapes of the American Southwest. This scenic route promises an unforgettable exploration of some of the region's most captivating natural wonders, including the renowned Bryce Canyon and Capitol Reef National Parks.

Starting your adventure on this byway, you'll find yourself immersed in a world of geological marvels and breathtaking vistas. Bryce Canyon National Park welcomes you with its surreal amphitheaters of colorful hoodoos, sculpted by the forces of erosion over millions of years. It's a sight that defies description and must be witnessed firsthand to truly appreciate its otherworldly beauty.

Continuing along Byway 12, you'll encounter Capitol Reef National Park, where the Earth's geological history is on full display. The park boasts stunning rock formations, rugged canyons, and the unique Waterpocket Fold—a 100-mile-long warp in the Earth's crust. It's a testament to the forces of nature that have shaped this region over millennia. The beauty of Byway 12 extends beyond the national parks, with scenic overlooks, charming towns, and opportunities for outdoor adventures like hiking and camping. As you traverse this route, you'll be surrounded by the awe-inspiring grandeur of the American Southwest, creating memories that will last a lifetime. So, if you're seeking an extraordinary detour through nature's wonders, Utah's National Scenic Byway 12 beckons. It's a journey that connects you with the geological marvels of Bryce Canyon and Capitol Reef, making it an essential part of any Southwestern road trip.

When planning these connections, consider the time of year, road conditions, and your interests. Each of these scenic byways offers a unique experience, making it worth exploring even further after your Route 66 journey.

Planning Your Return Journey

As you start planning your return journey from Route 66, here are some essential steps to consider:

1. Review Your Route: Take a look at the route you've traveled along Route 66 and any side trips you've made. This will help you decide whether you want to retrace your steps or take an alternative route back.

2. Visit Missed Attractions: If there were any attractions, diners, or landmarks you missed on your way to your destination, consider stopping at them on your return trip. Route 66 is filled with unique stops worth exploring.

3. Balance Travel Time: Plan your travel time wisely, taking into account the distance you need to cover each day. Consider making stops at interesting points along the way to break up the journey and enjoy more sights.

4. Accommodation Reservations: If you have specific accommodations in mind for your return trip, make reservations in advance to secure your preferred places to stay.

5. Check Vehicle Maintenance: Before you hit the road, perform a thorough check of your vehicle's maintenance needs. Ensure it's in good working condition to minimize the risk of breakdowns during your return journey.

6. Pack Essentials: Make sure you have all the essentials you need for the trip, including snacks, water, maps, navigation devices, and any required travel documents.

7. Explore New Routes: If you're up for more adventure, consider taking a different route for your return journey. Exploring new roads can lead to unexpected discoveries and experiences.

8. Plan Stops: Identify potential rest stops, interesting roadside attractions, or charming towns along the return route. This can help add structure to your journey and make the most of your time on Route 66.

9. Stay Flexible: While planning is important, leave room for spontaneity. Route 66 is known for its unexpected surprises, so be open to detours and recommendations from fellow travelers.

10. Safety First: Prioritize safety by adhering to traffic laws, monitoring weather conditions, and keeping an emergency kit in your vehicle.

Remember that the return journey on Route 66 can offer a different perspective and new experiences compared to the initial trip. It's a chance to relive some of your favorite moments and uncover hidden gems along the iconic highway. Safe travels on your return journey!

Chapter 11: Route 66 in the Future

As you plan your journey on the iconic Route 66, the time comes to contemplate the return trip. 'Route 66 in the Future' presents you with an intriguing choice: retracing cherished memories by revisiting the route you've already traveled or forging new paths along alternative routes. This pivotal decision will shape the character of your return journey, allowing you to relive favorite moments or discover fresh adventures on the historic highway. Follow along as we explore the options and possibilities that Route 66 holds for your future travels.

Preservation Efforts

The enduring allure of Route 66 lies not only in its historical significance but also in the tireless efforts to preserve its legacy for future generations. As travelers continue to traverse the Main Street of America, dedicated individuals, communities, and organizations are working tirelessly to ensure that this iconic highway retains its unique charm and cultural significance. One of the foremost preservation efforts is focused on maintaining the physical infrastructure of Route 66. Many segments of the highway have been restored, repaved, and maintained to offer a glimpse into the past, allowing travelers to drive on the same road that once hosted generations of adventurers.

Additionally, Route 66 is lined with historic landmarks, motels, diners, and attractions that have weathered the passage of time. Preservationists are actively engaged in restoring and preserving these vintage treasures. This not only preserves their historical value but also enriches the experience for modern-day travelers seeking to immerse themselves in the nostalgia of the route. Community involvement is another key facet of preservation efforts. Local residents and businesses along Route 66 play a pivotal role in maintaining its unique character. Festivals, events, and initiatives aimed at celebrating the highway's heritage help raise awareness and funds for preservation endeavors.

Furthermore, Route 66 serves as a cultural and artistic canvas, inspiring a myriad of artworks, music, literature, and documentaries. These creative endeavors not only pay homage to the highway's significance but also contribute to the broader understanding of its historical and cultural importance.

In an age of modern interstates and rapid development, preserving the authenticity and charm of Route 66 is a labor of love. The collective efforts of enthusiasts, historians, and communities ensure that future generations can continue to experience the magic of this legendary road, connecting them to a bygone era of American travel and adventure. These preservation efforts are not merely about preserving a highway; they are about safeguarding a piece of American history and culture for years to come.

Changing Landscapes

Route 66, often referred to as the "Main Street of America," has borne witness to profound changes in the American landscape over the decades. From its inception in 1926 to the present day, this iconic highway has mirrored the evolving social, economic, and cultural dynamics of the United States. In its early years, Route 66 served as a vital artery for westward migration during the Dust Bowl era and the Great Depression. Thousands of families embarked on this highway, seeking a better life in the fertile lands of California. The highway's roadside motels, diners, and gas stations were essential waystations for these travelers, and they became emblematic of Route 66's identity.

The mid-20th century brought about a surge in automobile travel, and Route 66 thrived as a symbol of American freedom and adventure. The highway became synonymous with cross-country road trips and the quintessential American experience, with countless families setting out on long journeys to explore the nation's diverse landscapes.

However, the latter half of the 20th century saw the rise of the interstate highway system, which bypassed many small towns and communities along Route 66. This led to a decline in the highway's economic vitality as travelers increasingly opted for the faster, more direct routes provided by the interstates.

The changing landscapes along Route 66 tell a story of adaptation and resilience. While some sections of the highway were bypassed and fell into disrepair, others embraced their historical and cultural significance. Communities and preservationists rallied to protect the legacy of Route 66, transforming it into a destination for travelers seeking a taste of the past.

Today, Route 66 stands as a living museum, where changing landscapes reveal the passage of time. Travelers can witness the contrast between well-preserved segments that harken back to the highway's heyday and sections where nature has reclaimed the road. The evolving landscapes serve as a poignant reminder of the enduring spirit of Route 66, which continues to inspire adventurers, artists, and historians alike.

As Route 66 navigates the 21st century, it remains a symbol of America's evolving identity, offering a tangible link between the past and the present. While the landscapes along the highway may continue to change, the enduring appeal of Route 66 as a cultural and historic icon remains unwavering.

Future of Route 66 Travel

As we look ahead to the future of Route 66 travel, it's clear that this iconic highway will continue to evolve while preserving its rich history and cultural significance. Several key trends and considerations shape the path forward for those who embark on the journey along the Main Street of America.

1. Modern Navigation and Technology: In the digital age, travelers can expect increasingly sophisticated navigation tools and apps to enhance their Route 66 experience. GPS technology, augmented reality guides, and virtual tours will provide new ways to explore the highway's history and attractions.

2. Sustainability and Eco-Tourism: The future of travel is marked by a commitment to sustainability. Route 66 is embracing this trend with a focus on eco-tourism, promoting clean energy options, and highlighting environmentally responsible practices among businesses along the route.

3. Cultural and Culinary Diversity: Route 66 has always been a melting pot of cultures and cuisines. This trend will continue, with an emphasis on celebrating the diverse culinary traditions and cultural heritage found along the highway. Travelers

can look forward to sampling regional delicacies and experiencing local art and music.

4. Preservation and Restoration: Route 66's historic motels, diners, and landmarks are at the heart of its charm. Preservation efforts will remain critical, ensuring that these nostalgic gems continue to thrive and offer authentic experiences to future generations.

5. Community Engagement: The communities along Route 66 will play an active role in shaping its future. Festivals, events, and community-led initiatives will continue to bring the highway to life, fostering a sense of belonging and pride among residents and visitors alike.

6. Cultural Exchange: As Route 66 attracts travelers from around the world, it will serve as a platform for cultural exchange. International visitors will bring new perspectives and experiences, enriching the highway's tapestry of stories.

7. Adventurous Exploration: The timeless spirit of adventure will remain central to Route 66 travel. The open road and the promise of discovery will continue to draw road trippers seeking to explore the ever-changing landscapes and hidden gems along the route.

8. Educational and Historical Significance: Route 66 will continue to serve as an educational resource, offering insights into American history, culture, and societal changes. Educational programs and interpretive centers will help travelers connect with the highway's historical significance.

In summary, the future of Route 66 travel is marked by a harmonious blend of innovation and preservation. Travelers can expect exciting advancements in technology and sustainability, while the enduring cultural and historical elements that define Route 66 will be cherished and safeguarded. The highway's future promises to be as vibrant and captivating as its storied past, ensuring that the lure of the open road will continue to beckon adventurers for generations to come.

Conclusion

.conclusion, the "Route 66 Travel & Tour Guide Book, 2024 Edition" invites readers on an extraordinary journey through the heart and soul of America's iconic highway. As we've explored the highways, byways, and cultural gems that make Route 66 so special, it's evident that this historic route is far more than just a road. It's a symbol of American adventure, nostalgia, and resilience—a living testament to the ever-evolving spirit of the nation.

From the bustling streets of Chicago to the sun-soaked shores of California, Route 66 unfolds a captivating narrative of the American experience. The guide has offered insights into the hidden treasures and well-trodden landmarks that await travelers, ensuring that every mile of this legendary route is brimming with stories and discoveries.

As we look beyond 2024, Route 66 continues to embrace the future while cherishing its past. Preservation efforts safeguard its timeless charm, while innovation in technology, sustainability, and cultural exchange infuse new energy into the journey. The highway's role as an educational and cultural touchstone will persist, ensuring that Route 66 remains a symbol of unity, diversity, and the enduring allure of the open road.

Whether you're a seasoned road-tripper or a first-time traveler, the "Route 66 Travel & Tour Guide Book, 2024" serves as your trusted companion, providing the tools, insights, and inspiration to embark on an unforgettable adventure. As you set out to explore the landscapes, stories, and communities that define Route 66, may your journey be filled with wonder, discovery, and the enduring spirit of the American road.

Made in United States
Troutdale, OR
05/09/2024

19730411R10164